To: _____

From: _____

Date: _____

SALT IN
MY KITCHEN

By
JEANETTE LOCKERBIE

MOODY PRESS
CHICAGO

Moody Press, a ministry of the Moody Bible Institute, is
designed for education, evangelization and edification.
If we may assist you in knowing more about Christ and
the Christian life, please write us without obligation to:
Moody Press, c/o MLM, Chicago, Illinois 60610.

Printed in the United States of America

SALT IN MY KITCHEN

BIBLE READING: Colossians 4:2-6

Let your speech at all times be gracious (pleasant and winsome), seasoned [as it were] with salt (v. 6a, Amplified).

Take salt out of our kitchens, and what will be the effect? The finest culinary creation will be tasteless. Eating will be robbed of most of its pleasure.

Salt has other notable qualities besides that of taste:

Salt cleanses. The Prophet Elisha recognized this fact when he used salt to cleanse the waters (II Kings 2:20-22). Surely the analogy is plain. What is more refreshing than cleanliness? The custom of bathing newborn babies with salt was practiced by the Israelites (Ezekiel 16:4) and continues in some parts of the world today. We apply the "salt" of concern and love in bathing a baby, or cleaning a home to make it a haven after a day in the working world's grime.

Salt seasons. The Bible calls Christians the "salt of the earth," and warns against losing our "savour" that seasons the world. We should allow this spiritual "salt" to season our conversation and back up our Christian testimony. "Let your speech be alway with grace, seasoned with salt, that ye may know how ye ought to answer every man" (Colossians 4:6).

Salt deices. The layer of ice on the porch steps on a January morning is much like the ice-bound heart, hard as a rock from the impact of bitter experiences. Both melt beneath the application of salt: one, the literal commodity; the other, the "salt" of kindness and peace. "Have salt in yourselves, and have peace one with another" (Mark 9:50b).

Can you think of any better place to sprinkle this "salt" than your own kitchen? Or any better time than right now?

SHINY-EYED BRIDE

BIBLE READING: I Corinthians 13:1-5

Over the threshold into a world as new as the going-away outfit! New china and linens, shiny new pots and pans, new furniture—and new responsibilities.

Over the threshold into a world as old as Eden: one man, one woman. Two individuals "joined in holy matrimony," as the minister intoned in the ceremony.

Individualism is not submerged. You are the same you. Personality is not one whit changed.

God, who made us, knows the propensities in all of us for selfishness, for self-seeking that leads to many other happiness-destroying traits.

We would do well then to take to heart right from the 'carrying over the threshold"—the beginning of a new life —the far-reaching counsel of the love chapter of the Bible (I Corinthians 13).

> Love [God's love in us] does not insist on its own rights or its own way, for it is not self-seeking; it is not touchy or fretful or resentful (v. 5, Amplified).

Living by God's pattern you can assure a marriage that will be, as Evangelist John Linton entitled a popular sermon for young adults:

> A heaven in which to go to heaven.

BETTER THAN A TRANQUILIZER

BIBLE READING: Philippians 4:4-8

> Here is a last piece of advice. . . . fix your minds
> on the things which are holy and right and pure
> and beautiful and good. . . . and you will find that
> the God of peace will be with you (vv. 8-9, Phil-
> lips).

Surely there is no better psychological restorative than
this verse in all of God's Word. "Think on these things"
the King James Bible says. "These" refers to balance-re-
storing, nerve-calming thoughts.

Undoubtedly the Apostle Paul wrestled often with his
thoughts: thoughts of friends who had forsaken him, con-
verts who had disappointed him, his own physical discom-
fort, the uncertain future, the very real possibility of a vio-
lent death. Far from dwelling on "these things," Paul left
us a formula for triumphing over such thoughts.

His advice to the Christians in Philippi was, "Think on
what will uplift you, not on what will drag you into depression and despair." This was not winking at facts as they
were. Neither was his exhortation to "make the best of a
bad thing."

Paul knew the mental, emotional, physical and spiritual
value of such "thinking"; such "fixing your mind." Real
value. Not to be compared for a moment with the world's
panacea: tranquilizers.

> "Whatsoever things are lovely"
> Will crowd out the unlovely.

THE EARLY BIRD

BIBLE READING: Mark 1:35-39

There was a time when the words "early bird" had an earthy, catch-the-worm connotation. Today the reference to an early bird will more than likely pertain to the Early Bird satellite.

Regardless of the generation or season, one "early bird" can be depended on to break the morning stillness: the year-or-so-old baby, herald of the dawn.

This eagerness to start the new day may not be echoed by the average mother, tired by her yesterday. Nevertheless, the one who will surmount the weariness and "rise up a great while before dawn" (or a reasonable equivalent according to the family schedule) will be rewarded for her effort.

In the quiet morning hour comes strength for the day. In the recognition that we are more than flesh and blood, that we are spirit and soul, in the deliberate feeding of our inner self, comes power to overcome the turmoil and conflicts of the day. The minutes spent in reading God's Word, in prayer and communion with our heavenly Father, will be reflected throughout long hours.

Admittedly it takes grim determination to roll out when the alarm sounds reveille. But remember the words of Harriet Beecher Stowe:

> Still, still with Thee
> When purple morning breaketh.

This is the hour when clear-channel communication between the busy homemaker and her God will prove infinitely more worthwhile than any "early bird" system ever dreamed of.

THE MAKER OF ALL

BIBLE READING: John 1:1-4

All things were made by him; and without him was
not any thing made that was made (v. 3).

What does a mother say when she is confronted with
blatant atheism in childish form? What happens when
second-grade Jimmy announces, "My friend Phil is the
smartest boy in our class. He says 'God is made out of
chemicals' "?

Jimmy's mother is well aware of the strong admiration
her son has for the "class brain." How can she contend with
the problem of destroying blasphemous seed without alienat-
ing the friend? How can she plant good seed in its place?

Her answer came, as all such answers can come, from the
Bible itself.

"Jimmy," advised his mother, "ask Phil this question: 'If
God is made out of chemicals, who made the chemicals?'
You can go on then and tell him that *God made everything.*
Don't argue, son. Just tell him you believe the Bible and
this is what the Bible teaches."

One thing we can count on: the devil will assail our children. He will strive to plant seeds of doubt that "He [God]
is Himself before all" (Colossians 1:17*a*, Berkeley).

Being forewarned we can be forearmed. Consistent prayer
for and with our family is the best of all bulwarks. We are
indebted too, for confidence and assurance, to the hymn
writer C. F. Alexander for the words:

> All things bright and beautiful, all creatures great
> and small,
> All things wise and wonderful, the Lord God made
> them all.

9

AGAINST A RAINY DAY

BIBLE READING: Psalm 119:10-16

Thy word have I hid in mine heart, that I might not sin against thee (v. 11).

"I just can't seem to memorize anything," is a typical reaction to a Sunday school teacher's suggestion that an adult pupil commit some Bible verses to memory.

Contrast this with the zeal of a Chinese convert from heathenism in this missionary's story:

"My house has only a bamboo roof," explained the convert, "and when the rains come they leak through. I do not want the rain to leak on the Word of God. Rain cannot leak into my heart, so I write God's Word in my heart." The new Christian then demonstrated his ability to quote whole passages of the Bible.

He lived to see "other rains" rob him of the Bible. The godless Communists stormed through his country. They took his Bible but they could not rob him of what he had "hidden in his heart."

Who can tell how long we will enjoy precious freedom to read God's Word? Why not make the most of it. You can't memorize? Maybe you would like to try what other homemakers have found to be successful: Tack up a typed Bible verse where you will see it often in the course of a day. Put it above the kitchen sink or near the ironing board. Think of how you can lighten your daily duties and relieve the monotony by memorizing God's Word.

And you will, like our Chinese convert, have built a spiritual shelter against a rainy day.

SAND, STARS AND PROMISES

BIBLE READING: Genesis 22:13-18

I will multiply thy seed as the stars of the heaven,
and as the sand which is upon the sea shore (v. 17).

Traveling through the desert, perhaps pausing to filter
handfuls of sand through his fingers, did Abraham ponder
God's stupendous promise? Sand. He could relate this to
mighty numbers, as God had promised his nation would
become. But stars! What similarity could there be in the
number of "sands on the sea shore" and the stars visible on
even the clearest night?

Ah, but Abraham had never stood on Mt. Wilson or Mt.
Palomar viewing the heavens through giant telescopes. It
was never given to him to hear twentieth century scientists
speculate:

> It would appear there are possibly as many stars
> in the sky as there are grains of sand on the sea-
> shore.*

No longer do astronomers have any basis on which to
scoff at God's promise to Abraham. The Lord makes no ex-
travagant promises. Increasing scientific knowledge only
brings this into focus.

Like Abraham we would do well to "stagger not" at God's
great promises. Somehow we muster up faith for the less
significant needs. God is waiting to honor our faith in big
things.

The late Dr. Roland V. Bingham, founder of the Sudan
Interior Mission, grasped this fact amid trying circumstances. His theme song and battle cry was:

*Dr. Irwin Moon, in *God of Creation*, Moody Science Film.
Used by permission.

Faith, mighty faith, the promise sees and looks to
   God alone;
Laughs at impossibilities, and cries, "It *shall* be
   done!"

STEP RIGHT UP!

BIBLE READING: John 10:7-10

I am the door: by me if any man enter in, he shall
be saved (v. 9).

You arrive at the door of the up-to-date supermarket. It
swings wide open, apparently of its own volition.

Did you ever pause to figure out what makes it work?

Have you sometimes stood on the threshold doubting that
the door would open? Or are you the technically-minded
type of young woman for whom the door poses no mystery?
You're aware that by stepping on a specific area you acti-
vate the current that operates it.

More likely you simply accept the fact without question.
In doing so, you are exercising faith. Faith in an "electric
eye."

Apply the same faith—or logic—to the words of Christ,
who says:

I am the door . . . .

"Enter in," Jesus invites. There is no need to stand outside wondering if the door will really open. No need to
figure out by what process He will open the door for you.

As simply as the youngest child, on a shopping trip with
Mommie, stands expectantly waiting for the door to open,
you can appropriate the benefits of heaven's open door. Just
step right up!

I am the door, the Saviour said;
I am the only door.

SHUT THE DOOR

BIBLE READING: II Kings 4:1-7

Thou shalt shut the door upon thee and upon thy sons (v. 4).

How often in the course of a day, especially in summer, does the command "Shut the door" ring out. We shut the door against the inroads of insects, pets, heat (in winter, cold). Springs insure that doors will swing shut even when manipulated by careless or too-tiny hands.

The Shunammite woman in our reading today had a two-fold need to shut her door. A creditor had come to take her two sons as slaves. She shut *in* her two boys. She shut *out* the world around them. A crisis called for nothing less than intervention from on high and she had no intention of letting outside interests rob her of the answer to her fervent prayer. In her extreme need she gladly heeded the voice of Elisha, the man of God. The abundance of oil that God supplied met her need of paying debts.

We might well wonder what would have happened had she done everything else God commanded, but had left the door open. Distraction and possibly derision might have moved her to abandon the instructions given by the prophet. We can only speculate, but we do know that unless we deliberately shut out the world's noise there will be little chance to hear the voice of God.

> Lord, I have shut the door,
> Speak now the word
> Which in the din and throng
> Could not be heard.

> —WILLIAM M. RUNYAN

WHEN GOD IS SLOW

BIBLE READING: Psalm 103:8-13

The LORD is . . . slow to anger, and plenteous in mercy (v. 8).

A young mother answered a hesitant knock on the kitchen door. There stood her five-year-old daughter Janey, mud-splattered, eyes downcast.

Taking in the situation in one glance the mother said, "Honey! Whatever happened to you? C'mon, let me clean you up." And she swept the child into her arms.

The kind, warm tones of her mother's voice started a flood of tears. Between sniffs, Janey gulped out, "Mommie, *you're not mad at me.*" Then, as though the sun had been turned on, the little girl continued, "I prayed and asked Jesus not to let you be mad at me for getting my nice dress all muddy. I asked Him to let me tell you first that I didn't play in the mud. Really, Mommie." The big, tear-filled eyes pleaded for understanding. "It was that nasty car that splashed me *all* over." Janey's words tumbled over each other. "And Mommie, *Jesus answered my prayer.* You're not mad at me."

What might have happened if Janey's mother had been quick to rebuke, harsh in judgment? A child's faith (that her mother had fostered!) might have been shattered. A sensitive child might have lost confidence in her mother's sense of justice. Instead, a new bond was formed. In the childish mind Mommie and Jesus were akin in love and understanding. Sometimes it pays to be slow.

NO INFERIORITY COMPLEX

BIBLE READING: Psalm 111

The fear of the LORD is the beginning of wisdom:
a good understanding have all they that do his
commandments (v. 10).

A personable young woman, who came to know Christ
as her Saviour through contact with a group of committed
Christians, admitted:

"Never in my whole life, no matter what the situation,
had I ever felt inferior. I had money, nice clothes, education, position. I had everything that makes for poise and
self-assurance until I met a group of women *who knew the
Bible*. Before their knowledge of God's Word I sat humbled, almost envious, conscious of my own inadequacy."

With her confession, the new Christian became an avid
student of the Bible. Soon she too was a challenge to others.

Whatever the motive, feasting on God's Word can bring
only profit. How true are the words of the psalmist,

I have more understanding than all my teachers
(Psalm 119:99*a*).

You need never feel inferior in this age when the Bible
is so available and when modern versions make its truths
clear to the most uninitiated student. The Holy Spirit is
ready to be your interpreter, and you can inspire others
around you to want to know the Bible's wonders.

Other books may puff us up.
The Book of books will build us up.

SPOCK STYLE

BIBLE READING: Proverbs 22:1-6

> Train up a child in the way he should go: and
> when he is old, he will not depart from it (v. 6).

"Me? Train a pliable, impressionable, important human
being?" Does the enormity of this task cause you to ask,
"Where can I turn for help?"

The young mother who turns to the child expert Dr.
Spock will find herself in the company of some 14 million
others* who consider his nonfiction best seller the final
authority.

On the other hand, the mother who turns to the all-time
best seller, the Bible, will join the ranks of those who, from
Solomon on, have considered God the final expert on child
psychology and training.

Read Dr. Spock (and we do not by any means disparage
his work) and you are on your own as to how to implement
his advice. Turn to God's Word, and the Author, through
the power of His Holy Spirit, is with you every step of the
way. Often, in thrilling, specific ways, He will guide you
and show you what you need to know.

Who can better help you than the God who breathed into
your baby the very breath of life. He can give you wisdom
as you mold this young life for His glory.

By following God's guidelines you can be certain you are
training the child *up* in the way he *should*, not *would*, go.

Happy is the privileged child whose mother believes this.

*Dr. Benjamin Spock's book on baby care has sold over
14,400,000 copies.

STOOP LABOR

BIBLE READING: Philippians 2:5-11

He humbled himself (v. 8).

In some agricultural areas farmers have need of what they term "stoop labor." These are the workers who handpick fruit such as strawberries, or set out seedlings that have to be specially handled. It's backbreaking toil. Not many flock to this type of job.

How often the young homemaker, weary after a morning of "picking up" after a small child and wiping up sticky floors, complains, "I'm nothing but a 'stoop laborer,' and I was trained for better things than this!"

A little quiet reflection would bring to the mind of the Christian the One who voluntarily humbled Himself with no griping, no complaining.

"Let this *mind* be in you" (v. 5)—in you, Mrs. Homemaker—writes the Apostle Paul. The mind controls the reactions. It's the mind, not the "dishpan hands," not the tired feet, that rebels. It's the mind too that can make humble housework bring glory to God.

The right frame of mind can make a challenge of the most drab, menial job. But the wrong frame of mind makes a miserable chore out of the pleasantest duty.

Do you sometimes feel you're nothing but a servant?

If you will reread verse seven, you will find you are in wonderful company.

LOVE THYSELF

BIBLE READING: Mark 13:28-31

"Come over for a coffee break," invites a friendly neighbor. But the reply comes, "Not this morning, thanks. I'm not fit company. I don't even like myself."

This young woman had hit a crucial truth. How could she be good for another person when she was in a self-despising mood?

It would be a fallacy to suppose that anyone entirely avoids having such days. But take heart. There is a cure for depression. But it is not to be confused with the "pep pills" sold at the corner drugstore.

"Love thy neighbour as thyself," said the Psychologist of the ages, the only One who can, in an instant, probe the deepest recesses of the mind and heart.

"He could read men's hearts" (John 2:25b, Amplified).

Self-love is akin to self-respect. When the day comes that we are "down in the dumps," that is the day to get on our knees. We should pray:

"Lord Jesus, the devil is tempting me to believe I just don't count in this world. Please show me that I'm Your creation. Help me to feel I'm someone for whom You gave Your life's blood, that I am important to You."

What "mood" can last in the light of such a prayer?

And, your self-love restored, you can enjoy fellowship with your neighbor.

THE WOMAN GOD CALLS GREAT

What woman does not dream of being great, really great? Not merely to be called by the loose term, "the greatest." Not to be Mrs. America or Mrs. Universe, or even a benefactor of humanity (a Madame Curie, perhaps), but great in God's sight.

It is significant to us who are homemakers that the only woman ever designated "great" in the Bible earned this distinction in her home. Just for being hospitable.

She began by inviting an itinerant prophet in for a slice of homemade bread. He must have enjoyed it, for he never passed the house without stopping for more. This unnamed woman's hospitality was expanded to include lodging for the prophet when he needed it. Thus for all time she provided the prototype for the "prophet's chamber"—that blessed haven where preachers, evangelists and missionaries, weary of hotels, motels and travel, find a Christian welcome.

Not everyone is in a position to offer room and board, but there is warm fellowship in even a spontaneous, "Come home with us, even for just a cup of coffee," before the stranger goes on his way. And remember what Jesus said about giving as little as a cup of cold water in His name? (Mark 9:41).

Sharing the blessings of our home, even though we may not offer homemade bread, puts us in line for God's commendation. Isn't it encouraging that this kind of "greatness" is within reach of every one of us?

THE TRIAL OF YOUR FAITH

BIBLE READING: I Peter 1:3-9

Riding a train in the Pacific Northwest, a pastor's wife noticed a fellow-passenger with an apparently sick baby. Although the baby was of an age when he should have been holding up his little head, the mother continually supported it. The two women began talking and the pastor's wife received this explanation:

"We've just come from the Mayo Clinic. Gary is severely retarded from brain damage at birth." Next followed some unforgettable words, "I'm so glad God gave him to *us*. We will love him. He'll never feel unwanted."

The light in the mother's face made her new friend glad for the fortunate child. She contrasted this mother to many mothers of "normal" children who fretted and complained all the time.

God could trust this woman with a severe, lifelong trial. He could trust to her care one of His little ones: a child who would never bring home a report card she could brag about to her neighbors; who would never excel in sports; who would certainly tie her to long hours of continuous care.

She could take it.

Not the trial, but the attitude we have toward it, proves whether we accept it as from the Lord. Recognize that He has, in even such a trial, a purpose rooted deep in love.

That the trial of your faith . . . might be found unto praise and honour and glory at the appearing of Jesus Christ (v. 7).

Not now, but in the coming years
We'll read the meaning of our tears.

THE RIGHT TO BE ANGRY

BIBLE READING: Ephesians 4:20-26*a*

Be ye angry and sin not.

Psychologists agree, "Your children are *going to make you angry.*" So, let's face it. That spurt of anger, according to the experts, merely marks you as "normal." It takes the Word of God, however, to tell us how to handle this anger. "When angry, do not sin" (Ephesians 4:26*a,* Amplified).

This is a tall order for even the most well-adjusted homemaker. How to do it? Well, here is one suggestion. Consider, "Am I angry at Johnny, or at what Johnny has done?" The implication of Scripture is that anger in itself is not sin. Assuredly our sinless Lord was justifiably angry on occasion. Jesus was angry at *sin.* He did not "sin in anger."

If we can objectively separate the object of our emotions, the child, from his actions, we may have the right to be angry. We may find if we are honest that some anger will be rightly directed at ourselves. For example: A mother takes sweet little Mary visiting. The child "acts up." Mamma's pride is wounded. She lashes out in anger against Mary. Would you agree that the mother should really have been angry at herself?

Sensing the wrong, a Christian mother would do well to confess this, both to the Lord and to the child. Nothing will so mollify a child as the realization that grown-ups too need to pray, ". . . and make me a better Mommy."

THE TWENTY-FOUR-HOUR VIRUS

BIBLE READING: Ephesians 4:26b-32

Let not the sun go down on your wrath.

A young professional couple in New York take the above verse literally. They admit:

"Although sometimes it's way past our bedtime before we settle a difference, we've made this rule. We never say 'Good-night' to each other until we have cleared up whatever has caused strained relations during the day. Better to get it out of our system. Who wants to start a day with a virus of misunderstanding left over from yesterday?"

Wouldn't you agree that this is sound reasoning? Why cloud the morning horizon? Each day brings its own quota of human problems. No need to aggravate these by aggregating them.

An experienced minister has through the years offered God's cure for the virus of misunderstanding, bitterness and anger to every couple he has united in marriage.

"You think today that you will never need this advice," he tells the shiny-eyed bride and proud groom as he quotes:

And be ye kind one to another, tenderhearted, for-giving one another, even as God for Christ's sake hath forgiven you (v. 32).

This is God's prescription and, taken before bedtime, it is guaranteed to work in less than twenty-four hours. Neglecting any virus is asking for trouble and complications.

Would not this be a good night to try God's sure cure?

HEALTHY FEAR

BIBLE READING: Psalm 56:1-4

> What time I am afraid, I will have confidence and put my trust and reliance on You (v. 3, Amplified).

Your child snuggles close, whispering, "I'm afraid." It may be fear of the dark, fear of "something" lurking in the closet, or even an unnamed fear.

"There's nothing to be afraid of," you reassure the little one, trying to soothe his fears. But deep inside, you know there is. You have felt fear's chilling impact. Who has not?

Says the noted atomic scientist Harold Urey, a Nobel Prize winner, "I myself am a man who is afraid. All the wise men I know are afraid."

There is such a thing as a healthy fear, a fear that does something about the problem. Fear of an epidemic, for instance, leads to immunization. Fear of an insecure future keeps insurance companies in business. The wise man of the Bible, Solomon, said: "The fear of the LORD prolongeth days" (Proverbs 10:27). Surely this is a healthy fear, this reverence that leads to a right relationship with God.

"The LORD will give you rest from your fear," is the prophet's comforting assurance in Isaiah 14:3. So, while the scientists' fears are understandable, you can confidently trust your today and all your tomorrows to God. His security-filled promise can allay the deepest fear.

> Fear thou not; for I am with thee: be not dismayed; for I am thy God: I will strengthen thee; yea, I will help thee (Isaiah 41:10).

HEART LINE TO HEAVEN

BIBLE READING: Psalm 116:1-5

I love the Lord because He has heard my voice
(v. 1, Amplified).

Can God hear one little cry in the midst of the myriad
prayers that rise from all over the world at the same time?

This question has troubled many a believer.

Some years ago a dramatic object lesson settled this
enigma for one Christian. The scene was one of New
York's crowded beaches. An estimated million persons
dotted the expanse of sand. Transistor radios blared ball
games and jazz. Ice-cream vendors screamed out, advertising
their wares. Mothers yelled at their too-venturesome off-
spring.

Suddenly, in the midst of all this confusion and din, a
lifeguard sprang from his tower, his toes barely touching
the sand as he darted toward his light skiff. In seconds he
had rowed unerringly to where a life was in danger. While
curious persons mobbed the waterfront, he brought to shore
the near-victim of a drowning accident.

In all the indescribable hubbub, the lifeguard's attuned
ear had discerned the cry, "Help!"

Will the omnipotent God do less?

No! says the psalmist. God will hear. His ear is bent in
your direction. He will listen. To the trusting Christian in
need of any kind of help, there is a direct line. A "heart
line to heaven."

A PARTNER WITH GOD

BIBLE READING: Matthew 11:28-30

In a unique sense, a mother is a co-worker with God. A Christian nurse on duty in the delivery room of a large city hospital brought this comforting thought to a patient. The woman, undergoing long hours of pain-racked labor, was in near despair before she heard the welcome cry of her baby.

"My dear," the nurse had whispered, "try to think even when the pain is at its worst, that you are *a partner with God* in bringing this baby into the world."

The patient's tension lessened. A new glow shone on her face. "Oh! I'd never thought of it like that. A partner with God!" she exclaimed.

God is looking for mothers who will be His partners, who like the "Mothers of Salem" that we sing about, will bring their children to Jesus. How blessed were those little ones who were lifted up in the arms of the Saviour. But some mothers had first brought them to Him.

As the days and years go by, the Lord will continue to be an active Partner. He will share the burdens. He will guide with His counsel, He will provide help in ways often undreamed of, for the mother whose trust is in Him.

If it is true that "A burden shared is a burden halved," how doubly true this must be when Jesus is the Partner carrying a share of the load. And this is a partnership that nothing can dissolve, not money or distance or time—not even death.

When Jesus said, "Take my yoke upon you," He was inviting us to come into partnership with Him.

ALL THE FORMS OF LOVE

BIBLE READING: I John 4:8-11

I'd sing the character He bears,
And all the forms of love He wears.

God is love. The smallest tot lisps it. The great singers lift us to the heights of heaven in song.

I wonder, do we stop to really consider that God *is* love? God is the source of love, not only its expression. If He were less than the source we would have to look elsewhere for the fountainhead of all love.

God *is* love. The present tense holds true in every generation. If we could only say "God *was* love" how could we be sure He still is? "God *will be* love" could hold no hope for us today, so gratefully we acknowledge that God *is* love.

God's love takes many forms. He loves us in spite of what we were, or are, whether in thought, word or deed. He loved us to the fullest extent. He expressed His love by sending His Son to die for us. He knows our inner motives and still He loves us. So great is God's love.

After years of study in the deep doctrines of the Word of God, a doctor of theology declares unequivocally, "The greatest power in the universe is love. It can move where no other force can make a dent."

"It shall from age to age endure" wrote a condemned prisoner on his cell wall (from the song, "The Love of God"). While we glory in this truth, the happy fact is that God *is* love—now.

SUNDAY DINNER

BIBLE READING: Acts 2:44-47

And in their homes they broke bread (v. 46, Amplified).

The late Dr. Morris Zeidman, founder of Toronto, Canada's famed Scott Mission, seated at the dinner table one Sunday, remarked to his hostess: "Don't ever give up this practice of making Sunday dinner a highlight."

He then added this thought-provoking statement, "Wherever your children may go throughout the length and breadth of the world, they will always return in mind and spirit to their home and what it stands for—when it's time for Sunday dinner."

"Is a meal so all-important?" you may ask. Perhaps it is not the food served, so much as the atmosphere that counts. Warm hospitality to guests, sharing together blessings of the morning sermon and the choir, and the whole relaxed environment contribute to this atmosphere.

Dinnertime any day will be largely what the mother makes it. An unruffled, serene (though busy) mother-hostess can make the simplest fare an enjoyment. Her harried, frustrated, edgy spirit, on the other hand, will spoil the most sumptuous meal.

As the Lord Jesus gladdened the home in Bethany on many occasions, so will He warm and bless your home—any home—where He is not only "THE UNSEEN GUEST," as a wall motto suggests, but in reality the Head of the home, acknowledged and welcomed.

An effective daily prayer might well be,

Come into my home, Lord Jesus.

NOT ANOTHER BRAND!

BIBLE READING: Isaiah 1:16-18

Wash you, make you clean (v. 16*a*).

"Be discriminating. Buy brand-name products." These words scream out at the homemaker from billboards, radio and TV, newspapers and magazines. Manufacturers exhaust the imagination of advertising agencies in their efforts to expose prospective buyers to the wonders of their products.

Eyeing the amazing array of detergents on the shelf, the shopper sighs, "Not another brand!"

Is there a "brand" that will stand every test of the most discriminating homemaker? One which deserves all the superlatives ever imagined? A "cleanser" for the inmost heart, soul and mind?

Yes, there is. The Bible declares with profound simplicity, "The blood of Jesus Christ his Son cleanseth us from all sin" (I John 1:7).

"All sin"—big sins, little sins, sins of long duration, sins that leave deep stains, secret sins known only to the sinner and to God. This is the claim made by God's Word. And it carries with it a 100 percent guarantee.

Of course, as in the case of the much-advertised product, there are directions to follow if desired results are to be obtained:

"If we *walk in the light*" (a picturesque way of saying practice obedience to Christ).

"If we *confess our sins*" (prefaces "The blood of Jesus . . . cleanseth us from all sin").

"If we will *come and reason with God.*"

Then the promise comes: "Though your sins be as scarlet, they shall be as white as snow" (Isaiah 1:18).

NO FAIR-WEATHER FRIEND

BIBLE READING: Hebrews 1:10-12

For I am the LORD, I change not (Malachi 3:6a).

A number of years ago this incident was related to us by an elderly deacon who had been the grocery delivery boy for Charles H. Spurgeon:

Watching the weather vane on top of the carriage house of the late Charles H. Spurgeon, a cynic jeered at the great preacher. Referring to the carved bronze letters that spelled, "God is love" as the wind twirled the thin metal vane, the scoffer called, "I wouldn't want to worship a God who is as changeable as the weather."

To this Spurgeon replied, "My friend, you misunderstand. The message is rather that God is love no matter what the weather, fair or foul."

How often we are disappointed over fair-weather friends!

Family and friends may indulge in "moods." They may cause us to question their love or loyalty as their circumstances put them in various frames of mind. Not so our heavenly Father.

"I change not," is His comforting promise in a world where changes in every realm occur with kaleidoscopic rapidity. Sometimes more changes take place in one year than have in another whole century.

The writer to the Hebrews would likewise reassure us with this certainty: "Jesus Christ the same yesterday, and to day, and for ever" (Hebrews 13:8).

While modern theologians in some circles are presenting what they are pleased to call "A twentieth century Jesus" (at the same time averring that "God is dead"), our faith clings to the unchanging Christ of the ages.

> All may change, but Jesus never,
> Glory to His name.

FAITH PLANTS A PROMISE

BIBLE READING: Hebrews 11:1-6

Faith is . . . the proof of things [we] do not see and
the conviction of their reality (v. 1, Amplified).

It's an exhilarating spring morning. The air is just brisk
enough to make a sweater feel comfortable as you grub in
the winter-strewn garden. The ground is prepared. The
seed is carefully sown. You go gratefully into the indoor
warmth, a vision of summer flowers and luscious vegetables
in your mind's eye. You may mark your calendar, circling
the date and noting: "Today I planted . . . ."

Planting is the evidence of faith: "The substance of things
hoped for" though not yet seen.

In like manner God will honor our faith when we definitely "plant a promise" from His Word, in full expectation
of results. The "planting" is a deliberate act of faith, and,
as our reading for today states, "without faith it is impossible to please him [God]."

With the same eagerness that a gardener watches for the
first green shoot, a Christian can confidently look to God,
who will keep His immutable Word.

> In faith I planted a seedling,
> A promise from God's holy Word;
> In hope I watched the fruition,
> The promise fulfilled by my Lord.

SOMETHING TO DO

BIBLE READING: Ephesians 2:7-12.

Created in Christ Jesus unto good works (v. 10).

"Why does not the church do something about . . . . . . ?"
The critics outline a host of social evils as they repeatedly
ask this question.

Perhaps we must in all honesty agree that there is a sense
in which the criticism is justified. So conscious are we that
our salvation is "not by works of righteousness," that we
permit the pendulum to swing too far in the opposite direction. We forget the exhortation of today's Scripture
reading. Good works should normally follow salvation.

A phrase from the printed prayer outlined for an adult
education group reads, ". . . and teach us to put into action
our better impulses." In this connection, Cynthia Pearl Maus,
author of *Christ and the Fine Arts,* states, "Feelings give
drive to human endeavor. *Do something.* Otherwise you
are all talk."

Think! If for this one day, every Christian would act
on his Holy Spirit-prompted "better impulses"! If only we
would take time to make that phone call that would bless
and cheer, or bake that apple pie that would say "A Christian cares," or give an hour to help a harried or sick neighbor.

No one Christian can meet all the many human needs
around her. But in the name of Christ, each of us can do
something that will reflect our heart's belief.

Then the church will be doing something.

PATTERN ALTERATION

BIBLE READING: Romans 15:1-6

Let each one of us make it a practice to please (make happy) his neighbor (v. 2*a*, Amplified).

Neighbors, as well as friends and family, come in all sizes and shapes: short, tall, slim, pudgy. Obviously the same size pattern will not fit each one.

Likewise, in the realm of personality, a different approach is needed for effective communication with the individual person. Recognition of this truth will help prevent us from possible blundering in our Christian witness. And right in today's text we have the best of all reasons for trying to understand: acquiring the right attitude toward our neighbor ". . . for his good and for his true welfare . . . to strengthen him and build him up spiritually" (v. 2*b*, Amplified).

How often it would be easier to "use the pattern just as it is," to stick to our own ways. But we have the pattern set by our Lord, who did not please Himself.

What about that difficult neighbor? No size fits her. The reward of achievement will come (as it does to the fastidious seamstress who alters the pattern to fit) when this neighbor will say to you, "You were willing to put up with me. You took me as I am."

Only you and God may know how difficult this was many times. But it is this understanding, this submerging of "my way of doing it," that will reveal some degree of conformity to our divine pattern.

It will not be difficult then to point your neighbor to the only One who can shape a perfect pattern out of her life.

Home is a wonderful place to practice pattern alteration.

CAN YOU CLASSIFY YOURSELF?

BIBLE READING: Ephesians 6:1-4

Rear them [tenderly] in the training and discipline and the counsel and admonition of the Lord (v. 4b, Amplified).

Let's take a peek into the homes of two identical Christian families: the same number of children, fathers in the same profession.

It's breakfast time. Family "A" seat themselves in orderly manner at the table. One of the children asks God's blessing on the food. The enjoyable meal over, father "A" reads a portion from the Bible. Then, before anyone rises from the table, he commits each one, plus the missionaries the family is interested in, to the Lord, for whatever the day will bring.

Breakfast time with family "B" is hectic. Each member scrambles for what he wants. In haphazard fashion they come to the table. Father "B" can scarcely get enough attention to ask the blessing. No Bible reading and prayer ends the meal in this Christian home. No start for the day with a sense of God's presence to guide them through the hours.

Some years pass. Family "A" can point with joy to a medical missionary son in India, a daughter who is a missionary nurse in South America, and two younger members who are vitally interested in church and in witnessing for Christ.

Contrast this with family "B." One son brought heartache and shame to his parents. Not one of the remaining three has shown a sign of commitment to Christ.

Would we dare say that the start for the day, year in and year out, had nothing to do with the vast difference in these "same" families?

And how would you classify your family?

WHERE DO SINS GO?

BIBLE READING: Isaiah 44:21-23

I, even I, am He Who blots out and cancels your transgressions (Isaiah 43:25, Amplified).

Five-year-old Billy had a problem. "Mommie," he began, "remember yesterday I told a lie. You said if I asked Jesus to forgive me, the sin would be gone. Gone where, Mommie? Where do sins go?"

Now Billy's mother had a problem. Where *do* sins go?

She spied a small blackboard. "Billy, write something on your blackboard for Mommie," she suggested. He scrawled some lines and odd figures. Next she said, "Rub it all off, son."

When the board was again clean, she asked, "Where did the chalk marks go?"

"They're just *gone*," Billy said simply.

"That's just like our sins, Billy," she said gently. "When we ask Jesus to forgive us, He just takes the sins away and leaves us all clean again."

The sins are gone. Oh, the guilt feelings we would be spared if only we would appropriate this promise ourselves. The psychiatrists could, in many instances, "close up shop." Nagging guilt would no longer steal our peace of mind.

In some Muslim countries people make a practice of writing out a list of their sins. They then wash the slate and drink the wash water. They have never heard what Billy's mother made so plain that even a five-year-old could accept its truth:

What a wondrous message in God's Word!
My sins are blotted out, I know!

LITTLE PITCHERS

BIBLE READING: Philippians 4:9-13

What you have . . . heard and seen in me, that put
into practice (v. 9, Berkeley).

Child psychologists are finding out that babies have a
stored-up vocabulary long before they begin to say words.

How often have you heard an incredulous mother exclaim, "Where did he ever hear that word?" as a grinning
child tries out a new combination of letters for the enter-
tainment of his elders. He is a practical demonstration of
"the little pitcher with the big ears."

Obviously the toddler playing with his pull toy is actively listening to the adult conversation, storing up some
words for later expression. And how often will we hear
our own words later repeated to us.

Can we then safely advise any child as Paul instructed the
Philippian Christians? There is ample evidence that these
people were his special joy (v. 1); for them he wanted the
best that heaven had to offer. Yet confidently he could say,
"Those things, which ye have . . . *heard,* and seen in me,
do."

Paul was no egotist. It's not *his* dedication, *his* sanctifica-
tion he offers to share. It's his *secret:* "Not I, but Christ
liveth in me" (Galatians 2:20).

Whether we want it to be so or not, we are the only samples of Christianity that some people around us know. Not
only babies but older children in the home too will pattern
their Christian lives after mother's.

With God's help we can make this a safe practice.

FAIR EVALUATION

BIBLE READING: Romans 12:3-5

Not to have an exaggerated opinion of his own importance; but to rate his ability with sober judgment (v. 3, Amplified).

In Christian circles, as in the world, we find extremes in more than one direction.

"Don't think too highly of yourself," someone quotes, and the inference is, "because you're not so important as you may think."

Does such a remark make your self-esteem hit zero? If so, it is well to consider that the restriction is not against thinking highly of oneself. It is the extreme the Bible warns against: "*too* highly."

A woman who earns her living by cleaning other people's homes has found the happy center. "If I thought of myself as 'a cleaning woman,'" she explained, "it would do something to my personality. Cleaning is my profession just as writing is yours." She is a first-rate worker, always in demand, and she makes a good living doing something she enjoys—and doing it with dignity.

It's what this woman thinks of herself that gives her the right perspective. God does not expect us to be hangdog, apologetic creatures. We have the dignity we were born with as His highest creation. On this we are privileged to build, with the help of His Holy Spirit, worthwhile character.

> Thinking too highly is being guilty of haughty pride.
> Thinking too lowly is underrating what God has made.

GOD'S CERAMICS

BIBLE READING: Romans 9:17-24

As the clay is in the potter's hand, so are you in
My hand (Jeremiah 18:6b, Amplified).

To the uninitiated, it is a never-ceasing wonder that such
varied shapes can emerge from the potter's clay. From the
beginner with her crude attempts right up to the ambitious
creations exhibited by the expert in ceramics, pottery can
be fascinating.

But suppose during the process the clay becomes argu-
mentative, refuses to be shaped in a particular mold? Does
this sound "way out"? Unthinkable? Such an attitude must,
nevertheless, be deeply ingrained in the human thought
processes. Otherwise would God have brought it to our
minds through His apostle?

> Shall the thing formed say to him that formed it,
> Why hast thou made me thus? (Romans 9:20b).

God, our Designer and Creator, has made each of us according to His pattern, as individual as the snowflakes that
fascinate the most sophisticated scientist. Rather than la-
ment, "Why am I what I am?" would it not be more profitable to determine; "Since I am what I am, with God's help
I will make the best of my abilities and my talents."

We *can* be God's exhibit pieces (v. 23).

It may take a lot of grace to sing from the heart

> Mould me and make me after Thy will,
> While I am waiting, yielded and still.

But in the process we will attain some likeness of God's
Masterpiece, our Lord Jesus Christ.

MY MOTHER'S PRAYER

BIBLE READING: Proverbs 31:25-28

Her children arise up, and call her blessed (v. 28*a*).

After starting for school one morning, a teen-ager turned back for a forgotten book. She slipped in and overheard her mother praying. She listened, and heard: ". . . and keep Pauline close to You today. Guard her from temptation."

Years have passed. The teen-ager is a mother herself now. Tempted to "get busy with all the work there is to do," she recalls her mother's prayer. She pauses to pray for the "Paulines" in her own family. Why? "Because," she freely admits, "many a time when I would have deliberately strayed from the light of the Christian knowledge that I had, my mother's prayer would echo in my mind."

Nothing is more potent than prayer. It works where counsel and instruction have failed. It succeeds where these have only caused resentment. And how far-reaching is the effect on a child of hearing mother's sincere prayer.

Highly favored is the child who is brought up where this is a daily experience. In her heart will be more than a once-a-year sentiment in remembering a Christian mother. The mother, who may be far away, will yet be speaking.

This song still rings out its timeless truth:

My mother's prayers have followed me.

THE BURNED TOAST

BIBLE READING: Luke 9:23-26

Let him deny himself, and take up his cross daily,
and follow me (v. 23*b*).

The alarm fails to go off. In your rushing around to get
breakfast, you scald your arm with steam from the kettle.
The toaster doesn't pop up. "Burnt offering for breakfast
again, honey?" your husband quips. And after all your hasty
efforts he tears off to catch the bus without touching his
food.

To top it all off, you drop a favorite pitcher, smashing
it beyond repair.

"Oh, well, I guess that's just my cross," you sigh aloud.

But is it? Think. Do not the same little domestic trag-
edies occur in the homes of non-Christians? Don't they
also burn toast, break dishes, rise late and almost miss the
bus?

What then is a Christian homemaker's cross? Is not a
cross (in the biblical sense) always something that is voluntarily, deliberately carried with full knowledge of the
implications? And for Jesus' sake?

It might well be the silence that descends on a group of
neighbors when you mention the name of the Saviour. It
could be the mustering of courage to thank God for the
food before partaking of it in the company of those who
never pause to say "Thank You" to the Giver of all gifts.
It could be jeering or sneering. It could be the misunderstanding of others when you refuse to "go along with the
crowd."

One thing we can be sure of. However heavy our cross,
it can never compare with the cross that Jesus carried for
us. And one day, as a favorite old hymn suggests:

I will trade the old cross for a crown.

A GREAT CALM

BIBLE READING: Mark 4:35-41

Peace, be still (v. 39).

Some years ago in a summer Bible conference in Ontario, Canada, a dreadful storm arose. The thunder drowned out the program in progress. A howling wind tore at the tent. Torrential rain made rivers of the aisles.

Amid understandable confusion, while the audience took refuge by standing on the benches, a voice rang out. A tall, stately figure rose on the platform. In her organlike contralto, Madame Lillian Jones, famed Negro soloist, her voice transcending the storm, sang:

And there was a great calm.

And there was. Somehow the singing had a calming effect on young and old alike in that great tent.

This is what the Lord does for us in the storms of life: those sudden squalls of sickness, financial strain, frayed nerves, personal relationships that go awry.

Like the disciples we might be fearful that our little boat will sink; that the Lord has somehow forgotten to be mindful of our needs. He is not asleep. He does know. He does care. He will say, "Peace, be still" when the storm is at its height.

Our voyage lies beyond the brink
Of many a threatening wave;
The world looks on to see us sink,
But Jesus lives to save.
—JAMES McFARLANE

INSTANT BREAD

BIBLE READING: Numbers 11:6-8

This is the bread which the LORD hath given you (Exodus 16:15).

We are living in an age of "instant everything" and the bread and roll bakers are not behind the times in their product. Supermarkets offer a great variety: "homemade," "brown 'n serve," "ready-mixed" and others.

Never, however, was there such a ready-to-eat bread as the manna God provided in the wilderness. No cooking. No mixing. No stove to light. No baking pans to wash.

Without controversy, manna is a type of "the Bread that came down from heaven," our Lord Jesus Christ Himself. Likewise the manna speaks to us of the Word of God, instantly ready to feed to the hungry soul.

Back when they were preparing to leave Egypt, the Israelites were told to make bread without adding any leaven, which pictured sin. They couldn't even keep any leaven in their houses. The bread was to be pure, with no added ingredients. If you are a compulsive "fixer-upper" and like to add extra ingredients, you may understand. You may also ruefully admit it's usually no improvement on the ready-mix.

What a parallel to the present-day treatment of the holy Word of God. It is mixed with a philosophy that would humanize God and deify man, and baked in the fires of higher criticism, all in an effort to make it acceptable to men and women who will not accept God's unchanging truth.

Even so, the Lord still sends His daily supply of spiritual food: pure, untainted, soul-satisfying to you.

> Break Thou the bread of life, Dear Lord to me,
> As Thou didst break the loaves beside the sea.

ORGANIZED FOR EFFICIENCY

BIBLE READING: Ephesians 5:14-17

The children of this world are in their generation wiser than the children of light (Luke 16:8b).

"Organization will defeat disorganization every time," a speaker once said. He pointed out the danger to the free world of the highly organized efficiency of the Communist system.

Who would dispute the basic truth of the statement? Many a harrassed young homemaker, taking an objective inventory of her daily routine, has found that hit-and-miss, disorganized effort uses up much of her time and dissipates her energy without accomplishing much.

Sometimes it takes a husband to bring this into focus, as one did. Watching his wife make a bed, he announced, "That's where you use a lot of extra effort, honey. You run around from side to side as though you were in training. See! I'd make up one side completely then make the other." He is convinced, "Anybody could keep house in just two hours a day."

Be that as it may, organization does prevent confusion. "A place for everything and everything in its place" saves time and frustration.

"Redeem the time" (buy it back from uselessness), says the Lord who is not the author of confusion but of peace.

By putting this scriptural emphasis into our daily "homework" could we not salvage time? Find time to do the things that have eternal value? Practice Christian love toward a shut-in, spend time teaching our own and perhaps our neighbors' children some truths from God's Word.

Organization can mean good stewardship and good use of our time.

GO HOME

BIBLE READING: Mark 5:14-19

Go back to your family and friends and tell them
(v. 19*a*, Berkeley).

A woman approached a visiting evangelist in her home
church at the close of a service. "Rev. Millard," she began,
"I feel the Lord wants me to preach."

"Wonderful!" said the preacher. "And do you have a
family?"

"Oh, yes! My husband and our five children."

"Fine!" replied the preacher. "Not only has God called
you to preach, He's given you a congregation to preach to."

Visibly disappointed at his reaction, the woman continued, "But, don't you see? There are so many people perishing in the world without the gospel."

"Go home," Jesus said to the man who would gladly have
followed Him. This was a man who had experienced a
miracle in his own life. He had been freed from the power
of demons. The all-knowing Saviour realized the need of a
witness to the man's own family and friends. The call to
home missions is often not glamorous. How wonderful to
read that the former demoniac *went*, at Christ's command.
In his hometown, admittedly a difficult spot, he told his
story. "And all were astonished" (v. 20*b*).

Perhaps if the woman who so ardently wished to go into
the world and preach had exercised her gifts in her own
home, the Lord would have raised up more than one from
her home to go as a missionary and reach the unreached.

Witnessing—like charity—begins at home.

FOR THIS CAUSE

BIBLE READING: Ephesians 5:28-33

We are living in a banner-waving, cause-espousing generation. Enthusiasm runs high over a variety of interests: both good and questionable.

Surely no "cause" was ever so worthwhile for the individual, the couple, the family or the community, as the right relationship between husband and wife. Reams have been written on the subject, in magazines, newspapers and books.

Meanwhile, the Bible has by no means been silent on this issue. The Bible has the answers!

It is no accident or coincidence that the directive, "For this cause shall a man leave his father and mother . . ." is spelled out clear and plain. How many marriages have foundered on this shoal! Mrs. Newlywed continues to refer to her parents' abode as "home." Mr. Bridegroom fails to cut himself loose from the apron strings. And trouble brews.

When a Christian home falls apart—for whatever reason —the cause of Christ is hurt. So "for this cause," because we are members of His body, our earnest prayer from the first day should be, "Lord, make us as a couple worthy of our 'membership,' never bringing into our marriage anything that will hinder Thy cause, always remembering:

> From heaven He came and sought her
> To be His holy bride . . ."

THE MIXMASTER

BIBLE READING: Hebrews 4:1-3

The word preached did not profit them, not being mixed with faith (v. 2*b*).

The recipe lists the ingredients. You follow the directions for successful cooking or baking. Invariably heading the instructions are the words, "Mix together ...."

Certainly the average ingredient left on its own would not only be unprofitable, it would be unpalatable. Who would wish to eat flour, for instance, just as it comes from the package, or baking powder?

The "gospel ingredient" is the Word of God. No one will presume to dispute its worth, yet, according to our Scripture reading for today, the preaching of the gospel in itself did not profit the listener. Something was missing: the "faith ingredient," belief in God as the Author and Finisher of our faith.

Moses, for all his wonderful qualities, was prevented from entering the promised land, although he was permitted to view something of its glories from afar.

How infinitely sad if we should, after having heard the gospel, come short of "entering into rest" (the rest of sins forgiven, the Christians' "promised land").

The solemn warning comes especially to those who do have opportunity to hear the Word preached. We might liken this to our having all the ingredients lined up and the electric mixer standing in readiness. But one thing must still be done. The power must be turned on.

Faith sets the "mixmaster" in motion.

ROOTED AND FRUITFUL

BIBLE READING: Colossians 2:6-10

Have the roots [of your being] firmly and deeply planted [in Him] (v. 7a, Amplified).

Some years ago in England, a prolonged drought struck an area noted for its luscious grapes. Growers despaired as the orchards showed dried-up clusters of abnormally small fruit. In the same area, one grape arbor bore fruit abundantly. Large bunches of purple grapes weighed down the arched boughs.

The secret? Far below the sun-crusted earth, the roots reached down to a spring that provided all the water the vines needed—and more. Significantly, the abundant crop came from the "King's Vine." The deep spring was located in the palace confines.

Drought—spiritual drought—prevents many a Christian from producing the "fruit of the Spirit" while, for the reaching, the spring water is available. Jesus, the King of kings offers, "If any man thirst, let him come unto me" (John 7:37).

Christ is Himself the living water. In Him is a constant, never-failing supply of spiritual life. Reaching deep, our lives will produce "fruit" as enticing to those around us as a bunch of luscious grapes.

We will never experience times of "drought disaster," nor will we have "off-seasons" when we produce nothing at all. Happily we will sing:

> I'm drinking at the springs of living water,
> Oh wonderful and bountiful supply.

PRESERVE US!

BIBLE READING: Psalm 16

> Preserve me, O God: for in thee do I put my trust
> (v. 1).

We learn early in life that "self-preservation is the first law of nature," not only in man, but in the lower levels of creation.

Preserving has its place of importance in many areas of the home, even though we may have passed the day when "preserving time" was practically a rite. We are vitally interested in "preserving the right of the individual," and we strive to "preserve the peace."

But when we come to the area of the soul we must cry out with the psalmist, "Preserve me, O God! I can preserve some things. I cannot preserve myself."

Nothing available in the world's market can be trusted to preserve our never-dying soul. "In thee do I put my trust," we say with David. With God's preservation there is not a chance of failure. "Having this seal, The Lord knoweth them that are his," (II Timothy 2:19). "The LORD shall preserve thy going out and thy coming in . . . even for evermore" (Psalm 121:8).

Would you want to take a chance on anything less perfect? Not *self*-preservation. Preservation by God Himself.

MISSIONARY HOMEMAKER

BIBLE READING: Matthew 28:17-20

A missionary on furlough, with a twinkle in her eye that belied her serious tone, surprised her hostess one morning with, "I see your servant has brought fresh milk." Moments later, "I see your servant is percolating the coffee and popping up the toast."

A few other such comments brought an understanding nod from the hostess. Well she realized that some well-meaning but ill-informed friends felt that missionary wives "have it made" with national servants in their homes. This help often makes it possible for the missionaries to do what they left their homes to do: seek to win others to Christ.

It may be that the missionary reading this page, especially devoted to her, would gladly trade her calling—for today, at least—for a few hours in a modern, push-button, gadget-filled kitchen. And the joy of doing her own household work!

Instead she smiles a little at the thought. With her "help" come also the daily frustrations, plus bugs and bats and crawly things, food scarcities and a minimum of conveniences.

Our missionary homemaker is human—not superhuman. But she knows it is in the daily contact in the kitchen, laundry and dining room that the keen national really sees Christianity. She wins the household helper for Christ and has a built-in interpreter, all trained in the customs and mores of her own people.

Can a push-button stove, a five-cycle laundry appliance, a modern supermarket compensate for this joy?

"Help me to ever live with eternity's values in view" is the prayer of the missionary homemaker.

ONE AT A TIME

BIBLE READING: James 1:1-4

As thy days, so shall thy strength be (Deuteronomy 33:25b).

A Christian physician stepped into a hospital room where his patient had been long confined.

"Doctor," she asked wearily, "how long do I have to stay here?"

In a kind voice the doctor replied, "Just one day at a time."

Profound wisdom led this man of God to give such a comforting word. How much easier it is to tolerate anything for a brief period of time than to think of the days and weeks stretching out before us. Is it not significant that the Lord promised, not "as thy *years*"—or even weeks or months—but "as thy *days,* so shall thy strength be."

We do not receive tomorrow's strength for today.

How often do we reach the end of a day and sigh, "I can never get through tomorrow." But at the moment when the day's strength and energy are nearly all used up, it's pardonable to feel like this. The secret, however, is to keep in mind always, that with the coming of tomorrow, with its problems and disappointments, will come strength. "Tomorrow" will then be "today," and today holds the promise of strength from the unfailing source: "My *strength* and my redeemer," as David phrases it.

Like the manna in the wilderness, this strength is meted out to us just one day's supply at a time.

> Lord, for tomorrow and its needs I do not pray,
> Still keep me, guide me, love me, Lord, thro' each
> *today.*

THE COST OF LIVING

BIBLE READING: I Peter 1:15-20

"Ransomed" . . . not with some money payment of
transient value, but by the costly shedding of blood
(v. 18b-19a, Phillips).

If there is one topic that interests the average homemaker
probably more than all others, it is the cost of living. Other
things come and pass: sickness, food shortages, calamity in
one form or another. Children grow up and are no longer
the absorbing responsibility they once were. But "living
costs" are always a problem.

The Apostle Peter would call to mind for us the unparal-
led cost of our salvation. We live in days when kidnappers
demand huge ransoms for the release of their victims. Yet
we cannot begin to grasp the ransom price Jesus paid for
our souls.

Nor silver nor gold hath obtained my redemption;
No riches of earth could have saved my poor soul.

So wrote a well-known and loved Bible teacher, James M.
Gray.

The most sophisticated computer in the laboratory of the
scientist can never report what it cost God, in one great
transaction, to purchase redemption for "whosoever will."

In days of fluctuation, this is a fixed cost: the blood of
the Son of God, no more, no less. Our salvation was purchased nearly 2,000 years ago at Calvary, it is as efficacious
in our day.

I am redeemed, but not with silver;
I am bought, but not with gold.

FOOD—FOR FREE!

BIBLE READING: Isaiah 55:1-3

Bread of heaven, feed me till I want no more.

Bread. What would our daily diet be without it in the Western world? It is well named the "staff of life."

Many years have gone by since we have known the long "bread lines" of hungry people obtaining food without money and without price. In our prosperous North America abundance is our normal lot.

But there is a "bread" without which we can never live eternally, and which we can never buy. It is free: a gift from God.

"I'll never take a handout" is the attitude of some who will not accept God's bread from heaven: His free salvation. It is free to us, though priced out of reach of any being on earth. All we need to qualify for this bounty is to admit hunger and the consciousness that we have nothing with which to pay for it.

Honesty demands that we admit, "Every good and perfect gift comes from above." We have nothing of ourselves. Thus common sense will lead us to accept the finest offer ever made to man.

He that hath no money; come ye, buy, and eat . . .
without money and without price.

The prophet's reasoning in verse 2 is sound economics. Why work hard and then spend your money for something that brings no satisfaction? Why, indeed? When Jesus waits to "satisfy the hungry with good things" (Luke 1:53a).

PRAYER IS——

BIBLE READING: John 14:12-18

I will do whatever you may ask in My name (v. 14, Berkeley).

Prayer is saying to God in this blasé age in which we live, "Father, I can't do it myself."

While advertisers almost wore out the phrase, "I'd rather do it myself," their emphasis served to pinpoint a modern attitude: self-sufficiency, independence, pride.

Prayer denotes the very opposite. Prayer is an admission: "Heavenly Father, I need Your help."

Prayer is kneeling on a rug marked: "Humility."

Prayer is believing: "*I* can't. *God can.*"

Prayer makes mighty warriors out of the weakest of us.

History records that Mary, Queen of Scots, trembled on her royal throne when word was brought to her that John Knox was on his knees in prayer.

Prayer makes even a child conscious of being close to God. This is demonstrated in the case of three-year-old Becky. Eager to "swim," she had her own way of obtaining a weather report. When her grandmother suggested it was going to rain, Becky paused in her tracks, looked up and said, "Dear God, please don't let it rain till we've had our swim. OK, God?" Later she referred casually to the weather, "It didn't rain, Grandma, did it?" Similarly, a five-year-old pooh-poohed a weather report that would upset her plans with "That man doesn't know. He hasn't even asked Jesus."

Prayer is far more real than direct dialing. It provides instant communication with the God of heaven. The God who *can.*

ASK YOUR FATHER

Bible Reading: Deuteronomy 32:6-10

Ask thy father, and he will shew thee (v. 7).

There was a time when, as naturally as breathing, you asked your father all kinds of questions. Some he could answer, and some brought the evasive, "when you're a little older. . . ."

Sometimes still beset with problems, you may feel the need of a father's counsel, consolation or loving advice. But it may be that distance is too great for the kind of communication that satisfies. Or your father may even have gone on before you, to heaven.

To whom will you turn for this unique fatherly interest?

Ask your heavenly Father. He is never too far away to hear. Never too busy to listen. In ways no father on earth, however loving, can meet your needs, God will undertake.

By prayer we can speak to our heavenly Father.

Through His Word He speaks to us. Have you known the thrill of reading the Bible and suddenly—as though it had just been penned that instant—a verse stands out on the page?

"That is just for me, exactly what I need right now," you will exclaim. God is communicating with His child.

> When God speaks, the sad hush their crying;
> When God speaks, the weary find rest.
> When God speaks, in sweet tones of comfort,
> With infinite peace I am blest.
>
> —Carlton C. Buck

There is no substitute, in time of trial, or when problems beset, for "asking your Father."

FREE SAMPLE

BIBLE READING: II Timothy 4:1-5

Be at it when it is and when it is not convenient
(v. 2, Berkeley).

Mrs. Jones opened her door to a smiling man holding out
a miniature box of detergent.

"Free sample, Ma'am," he offered.

"Thank you so much," Mrs. Jones accepted, then said,
"Just a minute. I have a free sample for you, too." She
reached for a gospel tract on a nearby hall table, and handed
it to the delivery man.

Whistling a tune, he read the tract as he went on to the
next house.

Would you agree that this is "being at it," being "instant in season"? And have you perhaps often longed for
a way in which you could serve the Lord and be useful to
Him? Has this seemed impossible to you as a housewife?

Why not have a supply of "free samples" on hand: a
number of well-chosen tracts. Keen publishers have made
available attractive titles specifically designed for salesmen,
insurance agents and neighbors.

Only eternity will reveal the value of distributing por-
tions of God's Word diligently as we associate with the
unsaved. Imagine your joy in heaven upon meeting people
you have reached with the gospel, whether it be your milk-
man, your newsboy, perhaps, or a member of the P.T.A.
Imagine being greeted with: "I might never have heard
about Jesus if you had not given me that free sample."

TROUBLESOME ME

BIBLE READING: Romans 7:14-21

My own behavior baffles me. For I find myself not
doing what I really want to do but what I really
loathe (v. 15, Phillips).

A wise woman once said, "The person I have the most
trouble with is the person I see in my mirror every day."

Surely this is an honest admission. What Christian has
not sincerely grieved over her own spiritual shortcomings:
over "doing those things I ought not to have done and
leaving undone those things I ought to have done" (to
paraphrase the *Book of Common Prayer*).

No follower of Christ was ever more acutely conscious
of this very trait and tendency than the Apostle Paul. We
might take comfort from this thought. But to allow ourselves to be trapped in Satan's snare—wallowing in despair—is to disparage the limitless, liberating grace of God.

Before turning introspective and self-condemning, and
dwelling exclusively on our sins, we might do well to note
a significant feature of Romans, chapter seven. Count the
I, me, my, and *myself*'s. Forty-seven personal references!
The Holy Spirit? Not once mentioned.

Let us then not linger in this valley of spiritual desola-
tion. There is a way to get rid of "troublesome you," or
"troublesome me." The cry, "Who shall deliver me?" (v.
24) echoes to the very throne of God. The reply, ringing
with triumphant deliverance and assurance, echoes to our
very ears.

There is therefore now no condemnation to them
which are in Christ Jesus, who walk not after the
flesh, but after the *Spirit* (Romans 8:1).

56

IT'S ALL IN YOUR HEAD

BIBLE READING: Philippians 2:1-5

Let this mind be in you, which was also in Christ Jesus (v. 5).

Few of us react favorably to the remark, "It's all in your head," when we seek sympathy for some ill we are suffering. Yet, more and more, medical science is finding a close link between physical health and mental attitudes.

Take the classic story of a woman who was so sensitive to fall flowers that she actually suffered a severe attack of asthma at the sight of a bowl of artificial mums and asters. It was "all in her mind."

In the spiritual realm the Lord gives much attention to our mind: our God-given power to think and to reason; the faculty that lifts us above all other creation.

"Be ye transformed by the renewing of your mind," is the injunction of Scripture (Romans 12:2*a*).

Our minds are going to be actively engaged, one way or another. The old adage, "Satan finds things for idle hands to do," can also be potently applied to the mind.

How can we prevent this? How can we "have the mind of Christ"? The Prophet Isaiah speaks to us of a mind "stayed upon the Lord," a mind filled with perfect peace (Isaiah 26:3). The head as well as the heart can be filled with the presence of Christ.

His "mind" is revealed in His Word.

GETTING INVOLVED

BIBLE READING: Mark 1:40-45

Jesus . . . put forth his hand, and touched him (v. 41).

Asked to define the difference between "pity" and "compassion," a woman answered:

"Pity 'feels bad' for someone in trouble or in need; 'compassion' goes a-visitin', taking along a pot o' soup or a fresh-baked cake."

Compassion leads to personal involvement in another's problems (even in this day of noninvolvement!). The Lord Jesus is our supreme Example. He "touched a leper." Who, in that day of no antibiotics, of superstition, of religious ostracism of lepers, would stretch a compassionate hand in their direction? Who but Jesus?

Can we fathom what that touch must have meant?

Pity would note their plight and possibly shake its head over it. Compassion made Jesus willing to become involved in their distress.

It is when sorrow or sickness comes that a Christian has the best possible opportunity for a real entry into the heart of a neighbor. With Christlike love and compassion, as we pray we will become aware of what to do, how best to help. We will "make the cake and go a-visitin'."

No leper is likely to need our outstretched hand, but we are daily surrounded by the lonely, the heartsick, the shut-in who longs for human companionship.

"Heartache is the most common experience of mankind," is more than a quotation from a sermon. It is a notable fact. Wouldn't this be a good day to get involved, to reach out a hand? And for our small effort, we will one day hear, ". . . ye did it unto Me."

RAGS TO RICHES

BIBLE READING: Isaiah 64:6-9

All our righteousnesses are as filthy rags (v. 6).

Filthy rags! The very sound of the words makes us turn up our nose in repulsion.

A woman attending her first gospel meeting was horrified to hear this expression "filthy rags."

"Not very nice language for a preacher to use. I expect something more refined from the pulpit," she protested. Later she humbly admitted that she had been shocked into looking into her own heart. Like this woman, if we have ever taken an honest inventory of what we really are, we will agree with the prophet.

It may be galling to our pride to note that it is our best, our righteousness, that appears to a holy God as revolting as a pile of unspeakably soiled rags do to us.

How dreadful it would be if we were left with this indictment and no way to change our situation. Oh, but there is! We can exchange the filthy rags for robes of righteousness. This is God's purpose and intent in unveiling to us our sinfulness: that He might provide for us, through the riches of His grace, all that we need to appear in His presence.

> Clad in His righteousness alone;
> Faultless to stand before His throne.

PRESSED FOR TIME

BIBLE READING: Ephesians 5:14-17

Wise people . . . make the best possible use of their time (v. 16, Berkeley).

Napoleon once said, "Ask me for anything but time."

How many of us would say "Amen" to this statement? In the course of a single week, how often do we say, "I haven't time. I would like to—but I simply can't fit it in. I'm too busy. I'm pressed for time."

Yet time is one thing each individual has in equal proportion: 24 hours a day, 60 minutes an hour. Each has 1,440 minutes a day to spend—or to squander.

There is possibly no more character-revealing exercise than to meticulously record how each hour in any given week is spent. Few who have practiced this continue to excuse themselves with, "I just haven't time."

Having studied what happens to their minutes, some have set about in earnest to "redeem the time." It is a sobering thought that we can never recall a single moment of time. The clock ticks on. The pages of the calendar are turned, never to be turned back.

How pertinent then are the words a missionary included in his prayer letter from troubled North Africa recently:

> Time is raw gold. Prayer is the mint in which moments are coined into heavenly wealth.

May each of us see the importance of prayer and be able to say at the end of the day:

> I was so pressured with the burden of things to do,
> I had to stop and take time to pray.

SAVOR THE FLAVOR

BIBLE READING: Ephesians 5:1-2

"And add just enough salt to bring out the flavor."

Flavor is what every cook aims for. Other things such as eye appeal, nutritive value and high or low calorie count are important. But without *flavor* we might as well take a nutrition pill at mealtime!

It's flavor that makes a husband smack his lips or that makes Junior beg to lick the bowl to "savor the flavor."

To the member of your family who has not yet "tasted and found that the Lord is good," you may be the only "flavor" of Christianity he or she knows. Whether or not this loved one will ever venture into a personal experience with Christ may depend on the flavor as he savors the sample you give him.

We cannot always rely on the excellence of a particular dish we concoct in our kitchen. We *can* be certain that with "just the right dash of salt" our Christian testimony will maintain its standard.

Asked what had first attracted him to Jesus Christ, a 70-year-old convert replied, "I liked what I saw in my own daughter, the change that being a Christian had made in her."

We can only give out what we have already received. It may be that time allows for just quick dashes of the "salt of prayer," a sprinkle of the "salt of the Word of God." But consistently assimilated, it will enable us to be the right flavor; to savor of the Christ whom we love and serve.

FANCY PHRASES

BIBLE READING: II Corinthians 12:7-10

My grace is sufficient.

The psychiatrist's terminology, meaningful to him, may sound like a "bunch of fancy phrases" to the uninitiated. One such phrase, which experts have used as they probe the reason behind some unspeakable crimes of our day, is "frustration tolerance." Extensive studies show that some of us are born with a greater ability to withstand frustration without building up deep hostilities (the real cause of antisocial actions).

Long before this day of emphasis on psychiatry and psychology, the Lord gave the Apostle Paul a solution to his frustration of a "thorn in the flesh." A condition so described in the Holy Land, where thorns are cruel in their pricks, must have been a perpetual sore to the apostle. It was no mere pinprick.

Paul took the first course open to Christians. He prayed about it. Not once, but three times. Was he emulating His Lord in Gethsemane, perhaps? (Matthew 26:44).

Not always will the Lord remove the "thorn." He did not for Paul, and the apostle was quick to acknowledge the reason for this (v. 7). But He will always provide the grace needed for us to bear our "thorn." We can even rise above the situation. Like Paul we can move beyond mere "putting up with it." We can actually glory in the trial, tribulation and suffering that comes.

Had not Paul come to this place in his life, we might not have been able to read today the comforting assurance, the simple phrase with a world of meaning:

My grace is sufficient for thee.

FOR REAL—OR NOT FOR REAL

BIBLE READING: Romans 12:9-12

[Let your] love be sincere—a real thing (v. 9a, Amplified).

Invited to attend a service for a young man being ordained to the gospel ministry, a supermarket manager replied, "Thank you so much. I'll be happy to come. I always liked that young man when he worked for me. *He was so sincere.*"

Sincerity ranks high on the scale of human values.

The word *sincerity* occurs only once in the Old Testament (Joshua 24:14),* and it is significant to note in what context it appears: The aged Joshua was making his final appeal to the people he had led for God. In a moment he would challenge them to a choice, but first he would impress upon them the solemn responsibility of such a choice. It had to be *real*: no pretense of serving God while they were in fact continuing to worship idols.

In a New Testament setting, "sincere" has been translated "pure," "unadulterated" (I Peter 2:2, Amplified), and this time it is in connection with milk. Can we imagine anything more deceptive, more dangerous than impure milk, the substance so depended upon for a baby's growth and strength? Well might the Apostle Peter lay stress upon "the *sincere* milk of the word."

How equally important it is then that we be sincere Christians, not deceiving ourselves or others around us. How serious is the pretense of being a spiritual Christian when one's testimony is not genuine.

"Let love [Christian love] be without dissimulation," the Scripture exhorts. In simpler terms, "Be sincere." Be a "for real" Christian.

*International Standard Bible Encyclopaedia, Vol. IV, p. 2804.

THE SELLING POINT

BIBLE READING: II Corinthians 6:1-3

Behold, now is truly the time for a gracious welcome (v. 2, Amplified).

You answer the ring of your doorbell. A saleswoman smiles and you invite her in. Skillfully she points out to you the worth of her cosmetic wares. She's too clever to try to sell you on lotions or potions. She sells beauty, glamour, compliments—and you buy.

Or what about a mattress salesman in your favorite department store. Noting your interest he immediately points out—not the number of springs and the yardage of cotton material—but the unexcelled sleep you can expect by buying his product. Relaxation traded for weariness—and you're sold.

Today's number one selling job is selling men and women on their need for Jesus Christ. God has all kinds of openings for all kinds of women: young, old, experienced, inexperienced, for full or part time.

And in the manner of the wise saleswoman, the Christian points out the benefits of "buying" and the evils of turning down God's offer:

How shall we escape, if we neglect so great salvation? (Hebrews 2:3a).

We will emphasize the direct advantages: sins forgiven, salvation for all time and eternity. We will enthusiastically "endorse our product" by listing the present benefits: peace of heart, the comforting sense of never being left alone, of being cared for by One who knows even the thoughts of our heart.

And keeping in mind that all selling is done by only 15 percent of the salesmen (the other 85 percent never

64

clinch their sales), we will ask the Holy Spirit for wisdom to lead our prospective customer to make the eternal decision: to "buy our product."

QUEEN OF THE CASTLE

BIBLE READING: Proverbs 31:10-12; 28-29.

Her husband boasts of and praises her, saying . . .
you excel them all (vv. 28b, 29b, Amplified).

Let's face it. Many of us are compulsive "joiners." We
become involved in one organization after another. There
is nothing basically wrong with doing so, and evidently
God, in creation, made provision for this instinctive trait.
He instituted the first group situation any of us has ever
joined: the family.

To this day no unit has ever occupied such a vital place
in society. Concerned, thoughtful professional counselors
attribute many a problem that besets our generation to the
breakdown of this first "social group."

Born in a hospital, early sent off to nursery school away
from parental influence, a child can conceivably go through
life right to the final burial almost untouched by a true
home environment. Yet home is, as it always was, God's
priority-rated institution.

Godless Communism would strike at the core of Christian culture by eliminating the home with all its depth of
meaning. The Christian wife and mother holds the key to
the continuance of her own faith: a key that opens the
door to a real home.

It is no coincidence that Solomon leaves to the last chapter of his "words of wise sayings" (Proverbs) a description
of a virtuous woman: a God-honoring mother. Reigning
over her home she wields untold influence.

If "a man's home is his castle," as the axiom states, then
you, Mrs. Homemaker, are the "queen of the castle."

A Christian home is God's best
Liaison between heaven and earth.

SOMEONE WITH A FACE

BIBLE READING: Mark 10:13-16

And He took [the children up one by one] in His
arms and (fervently invoked a) blessing, placing
His hands upon them (v. 16, Amplified).

How many young mothers have voiced the wistful desire
to have been among those favored women who lived, as
Jemima Luke so beautifully puts it,

When Jesus was here among men,
How He called little children as lambs to His fold.

Some such thought must have been in the mind of five-
year-old Janey as she knelt for her bedtime prayers.

"Mommie, I would like a Jesus with a face," she said.
"I talk to Him, but I can't see Him. I can't hear Him if
He talks to me."

And Janey's Mommie, listening, recalled something her
pastor had said some weeks before when she and her husband had presented their new baby in a public dedication.

"You will be the only 'Jesus,' the only 'God' this little
one will know for many a day."

It had seemed such a well-expressed sentiment at the
time. Now Janey's mother caught something of the real
import of her pastor's counsel.

To be the image of Jesus to a child whom we are eager
to interest in a loving Saviour: what a solemn responsibility! To stand in the place of Christ in the eyes of one
who will form his opinion of Christ by the image that
you and I—professed Christians—project.

A responsibility? Yes! And a privilege.

DOUBLE-TALK

BIBLE READING: I John 2:4-10

He that *saith* (v. 4*a*).

A stranger arrived in a small town.

"Where will I find Dr. Smith?" he inquired.

"Which one?" the resident asked. "We have two Dr. Smiths. Do you mean the one who *preaches* or the one who *practices*?"

We would do well to ask ourselves which Dr. Smith we are like.

It should bring some consolation to us to know that this failure to live by our words does not belong exclusively to the twentieth century. The first century had its quota of less than admirable saints, according to the Apostle John. "Talk is cheap," we might paraphrase his words.

> *Whoever says* I know Him . . . but fails to . . . obey . . . is a liar, and the Truth [of the Gospel] is not in him (v. 4, Amplified).

> *Whoever says* he abides in Him ought . . . to walk and conduct himself in the same way in which He walked and conducted Himself (v. 6).

> *Whoever says* he is in the Light and [yet] hates his brother . . . is in darkness (v. 9).

To be known as one who is "all talk" is quite an indictment.

By contrast, might we not rather be described as "she doesn't talk so much but you can tell she is a genuine Christian."

There is absolutely no better witness to the reality of the power of God than a believer whose daily conduct bears out his profession of faith.

Our prayer might well be, as we face each new day:

Lord, help me as a Christian to "practice what I preach."

A HOME TO WORSHIP

BIBLE READING: Colossians 3:1-4

During a prayer meeting being held in connection with a revival crusade, the woman in whose home the group had met became upset. The pastor, in an effort to comfort the lady, asked the source of her trouble.

Through her tears the hostess confessed: "The evangelist has been preaching about the second coming of the Lord." She gulped, then burst out with, "I don't want the Lord to come soon. Jim and I have struggled and saved ever since we were married to buy this lovely home. Now I want to enjoy it for a few years."

Is there perhaps a faint echo of these words in your heart as you consider your own reaction to a sermon on the blessed hope of the church?

A beautiful earthly home! With little thought of the home that Jesus has gone to prepare for us (John 14:2-3). And what of the certain promise of verse 4 of today's Scripture:

> When Christ Who is our life appears, then you also
> will appear with Him in . . . glory.

Is not then the crux of the matter, "Christ our life"? Not things. Not the lovely new home or the elegant automobile. Not any of the objects on which we have "set our affections," but the Lord Jesus Himself. *He* is our life.

> We shall see His lovely face
> Some bright golden morning.

In the meantime, as we "aim at and seek the [rich, eternal treasures] that are above, where Christ is" (v. 1, Amplified), the most treasured possessions of earth will fade.

FROM MY KITCHEN WINDOW

BIBLE READING: I Timothy 6:6-9

Godliness with contentment is great gain (v. 6).

Why do modern home planners so often have huge picture windows in the living room and allow for only midget-sized kitchen windows?

The comfortable farm-type home of another generation boasted kitchen windows that framed the landscape. Tired eyes feasted on God's unexcelled masterpieces.

It may be that today's homemaker would see little out her window but dreary brick walls, or possibly fences bordering diminutive back lawns. But the Christian always views the world through God's "picture window." The eyes of the soul can see through it:

The herald of spring in the stunted dandelion.

The border of perennials, speaking of God's year-by-year unfailing goodness.

The season-marking leaves, flamboyant in their autumn dress.

Snow that falls silently covering everything in a carpet of white, reminding the onlooker of the One who cleanses white as snow.

The window may be small, but it cannot limit the outlook. Only discontent can do this.

The Apostle Paul doubtless did not have much of a view from his prison cell, yet it was from this unlikely situation he evaluated his gains: godliness and contentment.

Like the kitchen window, the windows of the soul frequently need to be "shined up" for clarity of vision.

A GLIMPSE IN GOD'S MIRROR

BIBLE READING: II Corinthians 3:17-18

A particularly plain servant girl once worked in a home which contained many lovely art objects. Among these, a statue mounted on a stairway alcove captivated the girl. As she went about her work she paused often to gaze at it. After some time, the lady of the house was heard to remark: "I declare, that girl is beginning to be almost as beautiful as the one on the statue she admires so much!"

That "we tend to become like the person we admire" is a statement that gives much food for thought in the realm of spiritual truth.

> As . . . we continued to behold . . . as in a mirror
> the glory of the Lord, are constantly being trans-
> figured into His very own image (v. 18, Ampli-
> fied).

Is not this the very purpose the Lord has for each of us who are called by His name? "To be molded into the image of His Son" (Romans 8:29, Amplified).

And how will this be accomplished? By the same principle that wrought the change in the servant girl. By consistent, daily "looking unto Jesus" in and through His written Word.

We sing the lovely hymn, "Take Time to Be Holy."

We would do no violence to the thought if we were to sing, "Take time to behold Him."

REACH FOR THE SALT

BIBLE READING: Leviticus 2:13-16

Have salt in yourselves and live together in peace (Mark 9:50b, Berkeley).

Salt plays an interesting part in historic covenants: so much so that "The Covenant of Salt" was a common Near Eastern expression. Indeed, the Arabic word for *salt* and the word for *compact* or *treaty* is one and the same. Many a treaty was made around the table with salt as an important ingredient at the meal. The participants having "shared salt" were forever bound in a covenant together.

How easily then we can interpret our Lord's admonition in Mark 9:50, His significant linking together of salt and peaceful association.

The "salt of the Word of God"—the blessings we share together as God's children feasting at His table—should forever unite us in harmony.

Does a lack of harmony threaten our Christian witness? We need but "reach for the salt." Turn again to the Word of God. Fill our lives with His peace.

Does discouragement plague you, with its accompanying spiritual decline? Reach for the salt. The encouraging presence of Christ, as revealed in His Word, will brighten your day, "banish the blues," and lift your spirits.

Does the uncertain future cast shadows of fear? Just reach for the salt: the comfort and sweet consolation of God's "Fear not, for I am with thee."

A pinch of salt makes all the difference.

TROUBLE, TROUBLE, TROUBLE

BIBLE READING: I Samuel 1:1-10

Out of a sorrowful soul she prayed to the LORD (v. 10, Berkeley).

Hannah had problems. Even though she enjoyed the love of a devoted husband, she was childless in a day when this spelled the utmost in reproach. Add to this the daily hurt of seeing little children around her, and the barbed taunting of a rival who was blessed with children, and we can readily understand Hannah's situation.

In our day she might try feeding all her problems into a computer. After a few moments out would come the programmed set of possible solutions. I suspect Hannah would be too wise to trust such a source. Her case called for higher than earthly counsel.

Who among us, in the course of a day or a week, doesn't come up against circumstances that cause distress, and frustration? Problems for which there seem to be no solution. Like Hannah we too have recourse to the only One who can—in every situation, however "impossible"—give the needed help.

We too can "take our burdens to the Lord, and leave them there."

Hannah could not possibly foresee the exciting result of her earnest prayer. Neither can we.

MEET MOTHER HANNAH

BIBLE READING: I Samuel 1:11-20

I have asked him of the LORD (v. 20*b*, Berkeley).

Hannah is one of the very few women of all time who could confidently say, "It'll be a *boy*," and happily knit the blue garments in preparation for his arrival.

God had heard her prayer. (Surely this is a lesson on specific praying. Not just, "Lord, give me a child," but "Lord, give me a *son*.") And Hannah offered her son back to the Lord for service.

Was this woman tempted, I wonder, to forget her vow once the child was safely in her arms? Oh, but think if she had failed to "hand him back to the Lord" (v. 28, Berkeley), if she had not placed this boy in God's hands. She would never have seen the day when her son was given the signal honor of anointing the first king of Israel, of being prophet and counselor to the great King David, of being God's man when and where He needed him.

Giving our children back to God (who gave them to us in the first place) is one sure guarantee that we are doing our best for them. Not trust funds, endowments or insurance policies for education, can ever take the place of "handing them back to God." We should make sure our children are ever conscious that God has first claim on their lives.

For such children, the future holds unlimited possibilities. And you, as a mother, can share in them all, as Mother Hannah undoubtedly did.

BUT WHAT ABOUT ME?

BIBLE READING: I Kings 17:10-16

The jar of flour was never empty nor did the jug of
oil give out (v. 16, Berkeley).

If we do not keep in mind the custom of the day of feeding strangers, we might think Elijah's request a selfish one
indeed. But in this case, providing for the man of God
meant keeping alive the things for which God's chosen nation stood in a day of awful idolatry and apostasy.

Gladly the widow went to get a drink for the prophet.
It was when he called to her, "While you're there, please
bring me a little bread too," that she reacted.

"Give you bread! Why, my flour bin's practically empty.
I was just about to bake a little loaf. You saw me gathering
sticks for my fire. And when my bread is gone, my son and
I will die of starvation. Give to *you?* How can I?"

Somehow she got Elijah's message. She must have caught
a glimmer of hope in his promise. "She went and did as
he said," and today we can read of God's miraculous provision for her needs. "She, he, and her household ate for a
long time" (v. 15).

"Make mine first," said the representative of God. "You
will never regret it," I think I can hear him say.

God operates on the same principle today. If we give
gladly of even the little we have, we too will find that the
flour and cooking oil will hold out. Our needs will be met.

Withhold, and the opposite is true.

The Lord asks us to give to Him so that He can bless
what we have left for ourselves.

PRESCRIPTION FOR PEACE

BIBLE READING: John 14:25-31

I give you my own peace and my gift is nothing
like the peace of this world (v. 27, Phillips).

Peace is something we may never know we possess until
it is threatened. The happy homemaker, busy with a life
that brings satisfaction, rarely pauses to ask herself, "Am I
enjoying peace?" We become aware of our sunny days
only in contrast to a storm. When tragedy in some form
strikes the home, that's when peace is tested.

Not all the peace demonstrations ever staged can contribute one degree to personal peace. Yet, this peace is
available.

How many of us dream of being named in someone's
will, of hearing, "You have been left a legacy"? To every
believer in Christ comes this bequest: "Peace I leave with
you . . . not as the world giveth" (v. 27). The world cannot give peace.

So while the offices of psychiatrists and psychologists
bulge with persons in search of inner peace and relief from
the pressure of conflicts, Jesus continues to make His offer
of peace.

"Let not your heart be troubled," He counsels, as He
competently dispenses the prescription.

In earlier days, God had issued His prescription through
Isaiah the prophet, as he wrote (Isaiah 26:3, Amplified):

You will guard him and keep him in perfect and
constant peace whose mind . . . is stayed on You,
because he commits himself to You.

God's prescription for peace can be renewed daily, with
never a minute's waiting in line.

THE MOTHER TONGUE

BIBLE READING: Proverbs 8:1-9

The opening of my lips shall be right things (v. 6).

How can a parrot taken from some far-off jungle learn to speak a brand of English? Where has the bird learned not only the words but the tonal inflections that amaze a listener? Obviously he is "parroting" the mother tongue, the voice that taught him the art of speech.

In this connection, a mission director attempted to visit the homes of prospective candidates regardless of their qualifications and references.

"They will be all their lives what they were in their homes," is his unalterable belief. "Home example and training will take precedence in influence over college teaching."

While we may know indisputable cases where this is not so, the weight of evidence would seem to be with this mission official.

The Psalms and Proverbs abound with references to the use of the lips and the tongue, almost always with a cautionary implication.

With Christ in our hearts, with Him as our pattern, we can say the right things. Oh, it will not always be easy. It will not be a case of "saying the first thing that comes into mind." It will mean, many times, praying as did David, "Set a watch, O LORD, before my mouth; keep the door of my lips" (Psalm 141:3).

And it will pay off in the lives of our children who "parrot the mother tongue."

THE MAKING OF MEMORIES

BIBLE READING: Psalm 77:10-15

Memory. One of God's most precious gifts.

We never entirely forget anything. Everything contributing to the sum of human experience is pigeonholed somewhere in the wonderful filing system of our brain.

Does this give the added meaning to the role of the homemaker and mother? Indeed, it does. Who, in the course of a day or week, does more in the memory-making business than the wife, the mother, the neighbor, the friend?

> Lovely pictures still shall bloom,
> Upon the walls of memory's room.

Conscious of the truth of this couplet, a young mother was busy working with her three-year-old in the child's "garden," when a neighbor remarked, "Planting some flowers, are you?"

"Yes," the mother answered, and added to herself, "and memories." The flowers would bloom and die, but the years would never dim a child's memory of the mother who had time to share with her. Just to play gardener.

What kind of memories are we making, we might well ask ourselves. At the close of the day would we be glad if we could erase some things we have said or done, things our children will remember?

Best of all, will they remember a mother who lived for God?

A teen-ager, seeing her mother discouraged to the point of tears, feeling that her witness for Christ was completely ineffective, said, "Mamma, don't ever forget that it was you who led me to Jesus." A memory to cherish.

HOUSECLEANING

BIBLE READING: Galatians 5:16-21

"Now the works of the flesh are manifest . . ."

The spring sunshine blazes in all its glory. As welcome as its warming rays are, it nevertheless reveals the winter's accumulation of soil. Although Mrs. Modern Homemaker is largely freed from the ordeal our grandmothers knew as "spring-cleaning," with its turned-out rooms and general upheaval, when the first sunny spring day comes the urge is still there!

In like manner, the "sunlight of God's Word" brings into the open (manifests) sins we would otherwise keep hidden. Once these are revealed to us, honesty demands that we do something about them. They fall into three categories:

1) Sins against our own selves: *Personal uncleanness.* These we might liken to the things we stow away in closets, that no visitor might view them (v. 19).
2) *Idolatry*: Sin against God, our Creator. Putting anything, no matter how apparently innocent in itself, ahead of God in our thinking, is idol worship (v. 20*a*).
3) The next 12 names we might call "sins *against society*." These sins are all too obvious to the rest of the world. Often they hinder our testimony as professing Christians (vv. 20*b*-21*a*).

"But I'm only human," we say defensively as we go on being a stumbling block. Rather than defend ourselves so, should we not welcome the sunlight of God's gaze upon us —and get on with our spiritual housecleaning, with the help of the Holy Spirit?

UNLISTED

Bible Reading: Luke 18:9-14

I thank thee, that I am not as other men [or women] (v. 11).

Where, in the category of "works of the flesh" will we look for sins not specifically spelled out for us? Oh, God knew there would be among us some who would draw our skirts around us and smugly say, "But I don't do any of these things."

To our mind comes the scripture, "There is none righteous, no, *not one*" (Rom. 3:10). And God has left plenty of provision in the homey little phrase "such like," (Galatians 5:21).

A profitable hour of our "housecleaning" time might be spent searching out the "such likes" in our lives: the thoughts, words, deeds that we know about—and God knows about. We may have to dig deep into drawers, or long—unused trunks. We may have to make a journey to correct some things (as our grandmothers climbed the attic steps to clean the farthest recesses).

We may find ourselves disposing of trash in various forms. "Such like" in our library, in our forms of recreation that demand too much time from one who claims to be more interested in the next world than in this one.

Honest appraisal of our "such likes" may conceivably add up to a heap of discards—and to a Christian who will bring glory to her Lord, delivered from "the works of the flesh."

The Christian intent on a fastidiously clean home might well make her prayer concerning her own life:

Search me, O God, and know my heart (Psalm 139:23a).

81

CONCENTRATING ON THE POSITIVE

BIBLE READING: Matthew 12:43-45

Have you ever tried to find out your nonchurchgoing neighbor's estimate of a Christian? All too often she has only one concept: "A Christian doesn't do this. A Christian doesn't go there."

Somehow, as a group, we have created a negative impression. We are far better known for what we don't do than for all the blessings we enjoy as children of God and heirs with Christ.

It would be well, then, now that we have done our spiritual housecleaning, to determine what we will set out to accomplish as committed Christians. Are we going to be like the man with the unclean spirit we read about in our text for today? Are we going to be guilty of living an empty, useless, unprofitable life? Afraid to venture into the stream of life around us lest we get smudged and have to go through all the cleaning process again?

Surely we realize there is no such thing as static Christianity. That the inactive, negative Christian can never be an effective witness for Christ.

Will we then fill up the clean, fresh drawers and closets of our life? Make our witness count in new and fresh ways as we yield ourselves to the Holy Spirit.

There is no room for the *un*clean spirit (and/or his seven kindred evil spirits) in a life that is lived for God.

> Take my moments and my days;
> Let them flow in ceaseless praise.

THE MAGNETIC CHRISTIAN

BIBLE READING: Galatians 5:22-25

Let the beauty of Jesus be seen in me.

Some Christian women seem to have a magnetism about them. They have the ability to draw people—saved and unsaved alike—around them, like bees around a honey pot.

Can it be that they have followed through with their "housecleaning" more than others? Beyond the mere scouring and discarding and rearranging? Have they given themselves more to the adorning of which the Bible speaks?

Their lives seem as sweet and colorful and attractive as an array of peaches, plums, pears, oranges, bananas, grapes and apples—all arranged in a lovely bowl.

"The fruit of the Spirit." What a catalog of virtues! If we were to list all the things we would like to be, all the attributes we would wish to personify, we would have to turn to "the fruit of the Spirit."

Unattainable, you think? No! As high a plane of living as this seems, God has made it possible for us, by His Spirit.

It is "Christ in you"—not the spell of human personality, however winsome—that draws other people to our Saviour.

Has the fruit bowl become empty?

Or, perhaps the fruit is stale from lack of sharing it with others?

Wouldn't this be a good day to replenish our supply of love, joy, peace—and all the "fruit" that will make us magnetic Christians.

DEDICATION

BIBLE READING: Luke 2:22-34

They brought him . . . to present him to the Lord
(v. 22b).

Dedication can take many forms. It can be the simple yet
completely meaningful act of a father and mother who, in
the privacy of their own home, commit their child to God.

It may be a formal ceremony with special garments for
the baby, and the proud parents decked out in their Sunday
best. Even more impressive is it when other children are
included, the whole family renewing their vows to the
Lord.

Dedication is more than ceremony, however. Implement-
ing it is a daily matter. Dedicating sticky, messy Johnny;
stubborn, willful Janey.

With the prayerful commitment of children to Christ
must come the discipline of living for Him before them.
Here is one area in which we can help answer our own
prayers. We can pray not only, "Make him a good boy,
and her a good girl," but add to this prayer, "Lord, make
me the kind of mother I ought to be. Make me an example
of a Christian, so that my children will not become confused."

On that day when Mary and Joseph, with the future all
unknown before them, yet with a deep sense of mission they
did not quite understand, presented the Baby Jesus to the
Lord, did they also present themselves anew to God?

We read, "And the child grew . . . and the grace of God
was upon him" (v. 40).

What more would you ask for your child as you dedicate
him or her to the Lord?

FIGHTING THE JINGLES

BIBLE READING: Deuteronomy 11:18-21

Teach them [to] your children (v. 19a).

Dr. Benjamin S. Bloom of the University of Chicago, Head of the Research Conference on Education and Cultural Deprivation, in studies covering a period of fifty years, says: *"Half the intellectual capacity* of an adult has been developed by the *age of four, and 80 percent by age eight."**

Is this then the reason that God gave the directive (not an *elective*), "Ye *shall* teach . . . your children"?

Young children possess an amazing God-given ability to learn. The commercial interests have long recognized this factor. The glories of many brands of toothpaste, toys and breakfast food as well as definitely undesirable products are daily held up to the eyes and ears of our children.

What a wealth we could give these same children were we to take the findings of Dr. Bloom and other researchers to heart! The writer was intrigued quite recently by a pre-school child who had memorized verses beginning with each of the twenty-six letters of the alphabet. How many hours had this little boy's mother spent with him, as they sat in the house, when he lay down (for his nap), and when he rose up?

If this seems like too gigantic a task to ask of your little folks, it may be that for them *singing* Bible verses will be less difficult.

"I will sing of the mercies of the LORD . . . to all generations," the psalmist declares (Psalm 89:1).

This generation is our responsibility. We can so obey God's command that we will "sprinkle salt" that will preserve our children in the days to come.

*Quoted by Dr. Bernice Cory, Scripture Press, at the Christian Writers' Conference, Wheaton, Ill., March, 1967.

WHAT ARE YOU LOOKING FOR?

BIBLE READING: Luke 21:25-28

Straighten up and lift your heads (v. 28, Berkeley).

A man once saw a stooped, old woman on the street. He was told that when she was quite young she had on a few occasions found coins on the sidewalk. Ever afterward she walked with her head down, her eyes fixed in the direction of her hopes.

"Look up," the Lord Jesus exhorted His disciples—and us. Looking up is contagious. Did you ever try standing on a busy street corner and looking up as though intently watching some object? Isn't it true that before long others were similarly gazing up with craned necks?

Today trouble is surely stalking our world, and the hearts of men and women are "failing them for fear." The "four horses" of Revelation's prophecy are riding the earth, bringing war, famine, disease and death.

Christians are not necessarily escaping. We can bow under our share of the world's woe or we can (in the words of J. B. Phillips' translation):

Look up, hold your heads high, for you will soon be free (v. 28).

Seeing your confident trust in the promise-keeping God who holds the future, your neighbors may be drawn to emulate your example. True, they may not know what you are "looking up at," but this is your unique opportunity to share with them the truth of the blessed hope of the Christian: the coming of our Lord, and the need to be ready when He comes.

Lift up your heads, pilgrims aweary,
See day's approach now crimson the sky.

PLEASE PASS THE SALT

BIBLE READING: II Corinthians 4:1-5

If our gospel be hid, it is hid to them that are *lost* (v. 3).

Can you envision a scene in which someone sits at the table and hugs the salt shaker to himself, neglecting—refusing, perhaps—to pass it to anyone else! Salt, in itself relatively insignificant, makes all the difference between merely "getting the food down" and really enjoying a meal.

While practically no one would be so selfish, many of us must admit to having kept "the salt of the gospel" to ourselves in some degree.

Does the profound simplicity of our text for today strike a chord? Let's think about it for a moment. We have a precious possession. Other people who likewise are blessed are aware we have it. It's no secret to fellow believers. But to the neighbors around us each day, lost in their sins for lack of this "salt," our precious hoard is buried treasure, hidden from sight.

As the Apostle Paul states: "It is hid [only] to those who are perishing, and obscured [only] to those who are spiritually dying (v. 3, Amplified).

Spiritually "passing the salt" is no less than Christ has exhorted us to do. Will we then, today, be generous, and begin in large measure to "pass the salt"?

HOW TO PREVENT
BLUE MONDAY

BIBLE READING: Hebrews 10:19-25

Not neglecting our own church meeting (v. 25, Berkeley).

The cure for "Monday blues" has to be taken the day before, as recommended in our text for today.

"Oh, but I can worship God just as well if I stay at home," says one.

"I feel so worshipful when I'm out enjoying nature," another argues.

While both statements may be true of these individuals, we are accountable for what God's Word states:

Not neglecting . . . as is habitual with some, but giving mutual encouragement (v. 25).

Encouragement means strength for the week that lies ahead. Encouragement found only in the fellowship of God's people, around the revealed truth in His Word.

We return from the worship service with a sense of inner peace: a sense that, come what may during the week, we are in God's hands. It's a good feeling.

Besides the personal satisfaction of knowing we have been obedient to His Word and are in line for His blessing, there is another factor we should consider. By consistently honoring the Lord in His house on His day, we are throwing the weight of our influence on the side of righteousness in a day when this is sorely needed.

Like David we can sound out our conviction:

I was glad when they said unto me, Let us go into the house of the LORD (Psalm 122:1).

CHRIST'S YARDSTICK

BIBLE READING: Matthew 5:1-4

Happy are those who claim nothing, for the whole earth will belong to them! (v. 3, Phillips).

We all know such persons. The Christians whose theme song might well be, "I have Christ; what want I more?"

The world would rate them "poor" but by our Lord's yardstick they measure up.

These "blessed" Christians live as though they do not have a single unfulfilled desire, as though they own the earth. And well they might, according to the words of Jesus. Completely undemanding as far as material possessions are concerned, they are wealthy children of their heavenly Father.

These people are called "happy" (blessed), while many materialistic people, striving to "keep up with the Joneses," find they are never content.

Christ's beatitudes are often in disharmony with modern living standards, and yet are our timeless guide. It is for our own best interests our Lord would hold up to our view the things that endure, as opposed to the fleeting things of time.

We too can live by the yardstick of happiness.

OUR ALL-DIMENSIONAL GOD

BIBLE READING: Philippians 4:14-19

My God shall supply all your need (v. 19).

More and more we are hearing the expression, "the whole person," an admission that we who are God's highest creation are more than material, physical beings. Experts in the field of psychiatry generally agree that the true problems of our age are *meta*physical—beyond the physical.

The concerned physician discovers this likewise, in the increasing number of troubled persons coming to his office with a need for healing beyond the scope of mere medical aid.

Writing to the Philippian Christians, Paul shows his awareness of this all-round need of humanity: our need for more than just "three square meals a day" and shelter and clothing, important as these are.

There is provision for *every* need. God made us. He knows all about us. He is our all-dimensional God. What dedicated research teams seek today to find out in the interests of humanity, God has known from eternity.

"According to his riches in glory"—His unfailing storehouse; a continuing supply.

"By Christ Jesus"—He is our guarantee of a hearing, an "appointment with God" if you will. For Jesus said:

> Whatsoever ye shall ask in my name, that will I do (John 14:13).

We need only to acknowledge our need, ask in the name of Jesus and go on our way singing:

> Every need His hand supplieth.

DON'T STOP, PLEASE!

BIBLE READING: Daniel 4:18-25

It's time for family devotions. The children sit with their eyes glued on Daddy as he turns to the Scripture reading.

He begins, "Remember we're reading about the king with the big name, 'Neb-u-chad-nezzar.'" He carefully pronounces it for them and reads on. Then, at a climactic point of the narrative, he stops.

"Oh, *you wouldn't,* Daddy!"

"Please, don't stop."

The chorus around the table pleads with eyes and voices.

For them the Bible is an exciting Book, filled with living, interesting people and events.

Here is family worship that has meaning: Bible stories that enthrall, that will live in the memory.

Not all of us, of course, employ the "and - be - sure - to - be - with - us - for - tomorrow's - thrilling - installment" technique. There are other equally effective means to guard against the "let's-hurry-and-get-it-over" experience of all too many Christian families.

With the many readable versions available to us (the "Daddy" of today's illustration was reading from *Living Prophecies*), even the young child can understand and appreciate God's Word.

As we earnestly pray for meaningful ways of instructing our children, let us pray first of all:

> Make the Book live to me, oh, Lord;
> Show me Thyself within Thy Word.

Surely some of our eagerness will then be reflected in our family's desire to know and learn more about Jesus.

NO SPOT, NO WRINKLE

BIBLE READING: Ephesians 5:24-27

Overheard in a laundromat: "One reason I'll be glad to get to heaven is that, according to our preacher, there'll be no spots and no wrinkles. Just think! A world without ironing!"

This woman, though she may sound glib, is not alone in her thinking. "Wrinkle-free," "no-iron" fabric is possibly the most sought after kind in the store. Likewise, cosmetic manufacturers spend vast sums on research, and more (we suspect) in advertising wrinkle-preventing creams and lotions. Nevertheless, wrinkles are with us, alike in fabrics and in the human skin.

It is a comfort then to read that one day we will be entirely free from this ever present problem. The preacher is right. We will be gloriously changed. We *will* be without spot or wrinkle.

This is no highly rated advertisement. This is God's solemn promise. We will be like new. More than that, we will be new.

What is the "agent" that will bring about this transformation, that will sanctify and cleanse and make of us something glorious to behold, "without spot or wrinkle or any such thing"? The wonder-working Word of God.

As no demonstrator on earth, the Lord Jesus will one day present His "exhibits," the members of His church. By faith in Christ, by "using His product" we will be part of:

The glorious church without spot or wrinkle
Washed in the blood of the Lamb.

TIME FOR EVERYTHING ELSE

BIBLE READING: Haggai 1:1-8

Years ago you decided that your little church needed an addition, or that a new edifice should be built to the glory of God in your neighborhood. But somehow you always rationalized: "The time is not right."

Of course it's the right time for a new room to be added to your home, or to buy that new car (after all, aren't next year's models going to cost more?). It's just not the right time to make a move for God.

How often a man comes home from a church board meeting, all keyed up over a proposed project, and it is his wife who puts the damper on, saying:

"But, dear, do you think this is the right time? What about the cost? You know we have all the expenses of our own house right now. I don't see how we can give any more."

Multiply this response by half the women in the average congregation, and we can reasonably expect at least a postponement of the church project.

Meanwhile God is saying through His prophet:

Is it time for you yourselves to dwell in your paneled houses, while this house [of the Lord] lies in ruins? (v. 4, Amplified).

By contrast there is the woman who heeds God's exhortation, who puts her church ahead of her own interests. She is liable to be heard saying (following the board meeting), "Honey, I know we can give a little more."

For this Christian woman, "The time is right."

A TALENT TO BURY

BIBLE READING: Matthew 25:14-18

The sermon had been on the parable of the talents. The pastor had dwelt at some length on the "one talent" Christian, and on the way out of the church a parishioner said to him, "I guess, pastor, I must be one of these 'one talent' folks you were mentioning. I have only one talent. I speak my mind. When I have something to say, I say it!"

The pastor smiled and said graciously, "It may be, my dear lady, that if you give some thought to it, you'll realize this is one talent the Lord would have you bury."

"Speaking our mind" is all too often a source of satisfaction to the speaker rather than a way of serving the Lord with our talents. If the talent for "saying what she thinks" was channeled into service for God, she would undoubtedly be able to say words of comfort that would bless the hearer. Think, too, of the real satisfaction it would bring to her.

There is an emptiness that follows "speaking your mind," in contrast with saying what the Lord would have us say.

Speaking a word for the Lord—however ineffective we may feel our words to be—brings with it a glow that lingers on. This is a talent each of us has. We can invest it for wonderful dividends in eternity.

Today would be a good day to pray,

Let my lips speak forth Thy praise.

BUT MY *CHILDREN!*

BIBLE READING: Numbers 14:1-4; 31

All the Israelites grumbled and deplored their situation (v. *2a*, Amplified).

Real concern for one's children, as evidenced in verse three, is commendable. But how could these people have so soon forgotten the promises of God? How could they be so woefully lacking in trust in the almighty Jehovah?

Can we learn from their experience, that God is infinitely more concerned over our children than we can ever be? That He is abundantly able to care for them in any and every situation to which He leads us?

A Christian couple, parents of a teen-age son and daughter, were convinced God was calling them to leave a lucrative position to serve Him where the rewards and "security" were almost nil. They were heckled by head-wagging, would-be advisers.

"This may be all right for you, but what about your children," they would say. "Your brilliant son, your talented daughter? Do you realize you will never be able to send them to college? Their potential will never be realized because you're making this move."

Years passed and the very people who made these dire predictions witnessed the opportunities afforded the young people for whose futures they feared. Honors have been heaped on the Christian young man. His sister, like her parents, has done a phenomenal work for God in a distant land.

Our children—and we ourselves—are never safer, or more blessed, than in the place of God's appointment.

"SPRINKLING SALT" IN THE BIG CITY

BIBLE READING: Romans 12:14-18

Bless those . . . who are cruel in their attitude
toward you (v. 14a, Amplified).

In a crowded New York City apartment building, a
Christian woman was daily subjected to ridicule and scorn.
Neighbors, seeing her coming, would pick up a cookbook
and pantomime her hymn singing.

"When the roll is called up yonder," they would sing in
derision.

With unfailing good humor, Mrs. Jones just smiled.

One day a resident on the floor below her became
seriously ill. While other neighbors shook their heads at
the sudden tragedy that had befallen one of them, the
Christian spent long hours caring for the sick lady, taking
nourishing, appetizing food to her. She also asked Christian friends to pray for the dying woman.

Faith, diligence and long-suffering were all rewarded
when one day she stood with her pastor in that sickroom
and heard her once scornful neighbor confess her sin and
receive Christ as her Saviour.

Now this neighbor might truly sing, "When the roll is
called up yonder *I'll be there.*"

Mrs. Jones was a "salt sprinkler," sharing with those
who needed it the "savor of Christ." Soon more than one
in her neighborhood learned where to come for help.

"When the roll is called up yonder," many women will
answer, all because one Christian took to heart Romans 12.

Shall we, too, keep the "shaker" handy?

HOUSEHOLD HINT FROM A STAR

BIBLE READING: Colossians 3:15-17

> Hymns and spiritual songs, that are sung with a lovely feeling toward God in your hearts (v. 16*b*, Berkeley).

Here is a household hint shared by Lee Childs, onetime Broadway star and radio soloist:

"While I do the dishes, or some other work that doesn't call for concentrating, I often find myself singing and composing lines of a hymn."

A busy doctor's wife and mother of teen-agers, she takes her thinking time—her "meditating-on-God" time—when she can, and makes it both profitable and productive. This practice helps to keep her the "Sweet and Lovely" that was her theme song for many years.

God will give to each of us the same glow that makes Lee Childs a memorable Christian: the glow that comes from an inner radiance. The "song in our heart" will be audible. Unlike the Christian who said, "Nobody knows the joy I have 'way down in my heart," people around us *will* know.

The mundane things: peeling vegetables, dusting, the endless round of household duties, can be satisfying to the soul (as well as to the homemaker's pride) when the mind is engrossed in worthwhile thoughts.

With verse 17, "Whatever you may do . . . do it all in the name of the Lord Jesus," as our motto, how can we but think of Him? And thinking will lead inevitably to "psalms and hymns and spiritual songs."

WHAT'S THE USE OF WORRYING?

BIBLE READING: Psalm 37:1-8

Cheer up, ye saints of God,
There's nothing to worry about.

We sometimes sing these words but keep right on worrying.

Dr. Charles Mayo said to a patient, "I have never known a man who died from overwork, but many who died from doubt."

Doubt. Lack of trust. Worry. These are all in the same category. "Fretting," God calls it. And three times in the span of the eight verses we read today, the Lord exhorts us to "fret *not*." This is no arbitrary command or demand. It is wise counsel. Think for a moment. What does fretting accomplish?

It raises blood pressure.

It brings on tension headaches.

Is known to aggravate, if not actually cause, ulcers.

All this is on the debit side. Fretting has never been known to achieve any desired effect. It has no positive value.

Trade our fretting for trust and what do we gain? All the blessings promised in verses 3 to 6, even "the desires and secret petitions of your heart" (v. 4, Amplified).

"It's easier said than done," you may be thinking. Your mind may be hassling over a dozen or more problems for which you have no solution.

Verse 7 holds the tension-easing clue: *Rest in the Lord.* The Lord Jesus Himself invites:

"Come unto me, all ye that labour and are heavy laden, and I will give you rest" (Matthew 11:28).

What an invitation! What a promise!

MENU FOR MURMURERS

BIBLE READING: Numbers 11:4-6; 18-23

You shall see now whether My word shall come to pass for you or not (v. 23, Amplified).

A wise minister cautioned his congregation, "Be careful what you pray for. The Lord is just liable to give it to you."

The Israelites had mourned the loss of their Egyptian fare—and what a menu that was! Fish, cucumbers, melons, leeks and garlic.

"Give us *meat*," they griped day after day.

"Meat they shall have," the Lord told Moses. "Not for one or two days, but until they're sick of it."

How infinitely much better off they would have been if they had been content with the manna that, in mercy, the Lord sent fresh every day. But, no! They murmured and complained.

And we, if we will but admit it, often have to "learn the hard way," by bitter experience. Even with the exhortation to pray "Thy will be done," we still have to struggle with ourselves to really mean this. Yet it is in His love for us that God would plan our way and provide our needs. He alone can do this right. We can truly sing, "God's way is the best way."

Trusting Him completely, we will not pray for our own will and way—and neither will we have to live to regret our willful prayers. We will never have to become nauseated with a "menu for murmurers" we have forced God to give us.

UNDERNEATH WHAT?

BIBLE READING: Deuteronomy 33:26-29

Underneath are the everlasting arms (v. 27).

A young woman tried to hide her fears as she waved good-bye to her husband, who was bound for submarine duty.

Confiding in the lady sharing her taxi from the airport, she found comfort.

"I was fearful, my dear, just as you are. For you see, my son is a test pilot. I talked with my pastor and I'll always be thankful for the verse he gave me: 'The eternal God is your refuge . . . and underneath are the everlasting arms!'" (v. 27, Amplified).

This deep, consoling, comforting truth hit both women, the realization that there is *no limit* to the security of God's everlasting arms.

He is underneath the test pilot roaming the vast expanse of sky beyond our farthest horizon.

He is underneath the submarine in deepest waters.

He is underneath the child playing in his swing.

He is underneath the toddler taking his first halting steps.

The poet Whittier answers for us the question, "underneath *what?*" in his immortal lines:

> I know not where His islands
> Lift their fronded palms in air;
> I only know I cannot drift
> Beyond His love and care.

God's arms of love are underneath us—you and me—wherever we are right now.

FORGIVEN: TOO POOR TO PAY

BIBLE READING: Psalm 79:8-13

Remember not against us former iniquities (v. 8).

A young Christian woman, plagued with a sense of guilt over an incident in her past, went to her pastor in near despair.

"I can't forgive myself, even if other people could ever forgive me," she cried over and over.

In vain the pastor tried to assure her that God had forgiven her. Then he shared with her this story:

"I once knew a doctor who died with many of his patients still owing him money. On one of his big accounts was written, 'Forgiven. Too poor to pay.' The doctor's widow instituted proceedings to collect the amount anyway. The judge asked, 'Is this your husband's signature?'

" 'Yes,' replied the doctor's widow.

" 'Then,' declared the judge, 'there is not a court in all the land that can undo this,' and he decreed the account 'Paid in full.' "

Here is the glory of the forgiveness we enjoy as God's children. His signature forever signs and seals the transaction. Why then should we wallow in the despair that guilt produces? We *can* forgive ourselves, because God has unreservedly forgiven us. We need only pray, like David,

> Remember not the sins of my youth, nor my transgressions: according to thy mercy remember me for thy goodness' sake, O LORD (Psalm 25:7).

Then, although conscious that we are "too poor to pay," we can rest in the assurance that "forgiven" is written over our account. Nothing can ever change this truth.

HOW DOES IT TASTE?

BIBLE READING: Psalm 34:1-9

"Taste and see" (v. 8). A Bible injunction, to be sure. But it is also an everyday expression heard in the average kitchen. "Taste and see if I put in enough salt; taste to make sure the seasoning is just right."

Then there is the "tasting" that young Billy does when he licks the mixing bowl and spoon (if Daddy doesn't get it first!). This is possibly what the psalmist had in mind: "Just taste it. You'll be sure to want more."

Isn't this exactly what the concerned homemaker is eager to produce: something so tasty that one bite just naturally leads to a request for more?

Likewise, in the spiritual realm we might pray that as we mingle with our neighbors and friends our Christian witness will be "salted just right"; that the taste we offer of the good things of God will so influence them that they will want more.

We can be sure of the effectiveness of the "gospel ingredients." No fear on this score! Our concern should be that as we offer "samples for a taste" these will be so "attractively served" that the receiver cannot help but ask for more.

How eternally tragic it is to stop at "tasting the goodness of the Lord." The promise of blessing is for those who will go on to "put their trust in Him."

Think of how you first became interested in the gospel. The same approach, the same "sample" will certainly be used by the Holy Spirit to encourage someone else to go on from "taste" to "trust."

HIS MOTHER'S NAME WAS—

BIBLE READING: II Chronicles 26:1-5; 29:1

His mother's name also was Jecoliah (v. 3b).

His mother's name. Hezekiah, the king to whom the Lord added fifteen years of life. Who ever hears his mother's name? And the young King Uzziah. Who could easily recall *his* mother's name?

There is something significant in the mention of this mother of Uzziah. His father had "turned away from following the LORD" (II Chronicles 25:27). Did the young man then regard his mother and her faith in God as such a bulwark that he was enabled to "do that which was right in the sight of the LORD"? At sixteen!

It was the great Baptist preacher, Charles Haddon Spurgeon, who stood one day by his mother's grave and cried, "Oh, Mother, Mother! I would not have been the man I am if you had not been the woman you were."

You too are raising your boy with the help of the Lord, to serve Him, to "do what is right in His eyes." You cannot yet see where his path will lead or what his future will be. But you can be very sure you are shaping that future. Like the mothers of Bible heroes, we can pray, and counsel and live for God ourselves before our children.

Oh, it will likely happen that should that boy become a famous preacher, missionary, doctor or scientist, nobody will know who his mother is. But you will know—and God will know. And isn't that enough to make it worthwhile?

FAITH IN ACTION

BIBLE READING: Exodus 2:1-10

> She got him a reed basket . . . She tucked the child
> in it and set it among the reeds near the river-bank
> (v. 3, Berkeley).

Today's story is closely akin to yesterday's. A mother
unknown by name to the majority of people, whose son
was undoubtedly one of the greatest emanicipators of all
history: Moses.

His mother's name was Jochebed (6:20).

Could she have known, that day she committed her
three-month-old baby boy to the banks of the Nile (river
of death for Hebrew babies, 1:22) that this was a child
of destiny? To her he was "exceedingly beautiful" (Amplified), but then what child is not, in his mother's eyes?

Jochebed's faith cost her something: fear of the great
Pharaoh's wrath should her deed be discovered by his exe-
cutioners. Undaunted, this mother waited in expectation
of deliverance for her son.

God had a plan for this boy—and His plan called for
the cooperation of a mother who would dare to go against
the edict of a mighty, godless ruler.

The same Lord has a plan for your son or daughter. Civil
powers can make their decrees: No prayer in the schools, no
Bible to be read in certain public places. Anti-God fac-
tions can spew out their atheism. God is still the "God of
Jochebed." He will take note of our efforts to deliver our
own children. "Nursing them" with the Word of God;
"bathing them" in prayer, who knows? We may be en-
trusted with a "Moses"!

FIVE *SOMETHINGS*

BIBLE READING: John 5:19-24

"I have a memory like a sieve," laments a new Christian. "The only verse I've been able to memorize is John 5:24, and I don't always quote that right."

But, with her sievelike memory, she has a wise practice: she carries a card with the verse written on it, and when she has an opportunity, she draws it out.

"This has five 'somethings' in it," she tells her friends.

"He that heareth"—

something to *hear;*

"and believeth"—

something to *believe;*

"hath everlasting life"—

something to *possess;*

"and shall not come into condemnation"—

something to *avoid;*

"is passed from death unto life"—

something to *enjoy.*

By this time invariably the question is asked, "Who said that?" Who, indeed, but our Lord Himself!

Is this, perhaps, what Jesus had in mind when He said, "Ye shall be witnesses unto me"?

In such ways is the "salt of the gospel" sprinkled where it is so sorely needed to flavor a life (and to save a soul). We can all "shake some salt," even if we too have to resort to writing down a favorite verse. We can be confident that, whatever the verse may be, empowered by the Holy Spirit it will find its mark. Like no guided missile ever devised by man, the Word of God will accomplish its Designer's purpose (Isaiah 55:11).

All it needs is someone to launch it. Even someone "with a memory like a sieve."

DIVINE PSYCHIATRY

BIBLE READING: Hebrews 4:9-13

> For the Word of God is . . . skilled in judging the
> heart's ponderings and meditations (v. 12, Ber-
> keley).

The writer to the Hebrews had doubtless never heard of
"couch therapy" (as we know it). How then can he so
incisively describe the process?

Seeking out "the thoughts and intents of the heart" would
take many a costly session with even the finest psychiatrist.
Yet our Bible, with unerring accuracy, arrives at a speedy
diagnosis.

"The heart is deceitful," writes Jeremiah, "and utterly
corrupt" (17:9, Berkeley).

But who among us is willing to settle for knowing the
nature of our disease? We want help, treatment, a cure.

Here too the Bible is way out front. Jeremiah offers the
perfect cure for "heart trouble" that sparks our many ills
of body and mind.

"I will give them a heart to know Me, that I am the
LORD" (24:7). Add to this the words of Ezekiel if you
are the kind who appreciates consultations with more than
one doctor,

> A new heart, too, I will give you, and a new spirit
> I will put within you (Ezekiel 36:26a, Berkeley).

Better still, we can hear the Great Physician say to us,
"Let not your heart be troubled." And He prescribes, "Believe . . . in me" (John 14:1). Here then is the timeless
panacea, unconditionally guaranteed to relieve us of the
problems that bring crowds to the office of the psychiatrist.

IF ONLY I HAD ANOTHER CHANCE!

BIBLE READING: Luke 22:54-62

And Peter went out, and wept bitterly (v. 62).

Can't you hear Peter's wail, "If only I had another chance!" Who among us cannot share, to some degree, his feelings of bitter remorse? We too can recall incidents that make us wish we might have another chance. What we would do with it we will never know, for, as a wise man once said, "History does not reveal its alternatives."

Under the same conditions, in the same setting (without the knowledge that comes from 'hindsight'), we would probably do exactly the same as we did on the previous occasion. Otherwise why did we so act then?

The lesson would appear to be crystal clear: If we do not want to live in a world of regrets, of bitter remorse, had we not better consider carefully our actions each day? Ask the Lord for His wisdom and His daily guidance.

A woman confiding her troubles to a friend in a distant city wrote, "Will you please pray with me that, in this crisis, I'll be guided to do what, a year from now, I will wish I had done (or *be glad I did!*)."

Here is a thoughtful, mature Christian. She has honestly faced the possibility of making a decision that can lead to a future filled with, "I wish I had—"

We must take the right ounce of prevention, thus turning to the right source, for, said the Lord, "I will guide thee with mine eye" (Psalm 32:8b). With Him as our Guide and Helper, we can live today so that we will have no regrets tomorrow.

WHO IS MY NEIGHBOR?

BIBLE READING: Luke 10:27-37

There was a day when neighbors played an important part in our lives. Big, impersonal apartment buildings and "developments" however have tended to create less of a neighborly situation. Clothes driers have largely eliminated the friendly, over-the-clothesline chats. Even so, if we have to ask ourselves, "Who is my neighbor?" we are revealing our own shortcomings on this score.

The Scriptures abound with admonitions as to how we should treat our neighbors. (Jesus must have felt they were vitally important, He gave such specific commands concerning our responsibility.) At least nine times in the New Testament we are exhorted to "Love our neighbour." Wouldn't that imply *knowing* her? We can't love someone to whom we scarcely give the time of day.

Who then is our neighbor—this person whom we are not to talk against, whose goods we are not to covet, whom we are not to hate or slander, whom we are to "love as much as we love ourselves"?

Missionaries in a Southeast Asian country faced this question. Their mission was to reach Bengali-speaking people. "But in the meantime," they reasoned, "we have English neighbors" (professionals whose business firms had sent them there).

The missionaries were friendly. They invited the neighbors for coffee and chats. After many months they had the joy of leading both husband and wife to Christ.

"I had to come halfway around the world to find God," the husband confessed.

But find Him he did—because some missionaries answered the question, "Who is my neighbor?"

JUST LOOKING

BIBLE READING: John 6:35-40

If there is one thing the average man will never quite understand about women, it is the real joy we get out of "just looking" in our favorite stores.

"Why bother if you don't really want to buy something?" is the typical masculine reasoning.

Are there times, I wonder, when we are "just looking"; not really "shopping" for the will of God for our lives? When we pray our formal prayers, ostensibly "committing our way unto the Lord," but in reality not too interested in claiming any of His offers?

We may read booklets and pamphlets on the subject, listen to radio sermons on, "How to know the will of God," be able to present well-thought-out, pertinent points when the subject is discussed. But we are "just looking." Just passing an interesting half hour.

Like the shopper who doesn't buy, we don't need the item we're inspecting on the counter or shelf. Or, other factors may enter in: We may not recognize our need, or "the price" may not be right. In the matter of God's will for us, the price might be an unwanted change of location, status or income. It could be that we do want the will of God—but we don't want it just yet. We're content for the time being; hesitant about any uncertain, unpredictable move.

So, all too often many of us go on "just looking" when we might be enjoying all that God has to offer from His storehouse of promises. The price? A sincere prayer: "Not my will but Thine be done."

WHERE CAN WE GO?

BIBLE READING: John 6:63-68

And his disciples came . . . and told Jesus (Matthew 14:12).

"Where we go" is often revelatory of "what or whom we *know*."

A homey little illustration along this line comes from a farmer's son. Jimmy could always be counted on to find the lost cow, even when others had given up. Asked "How do you do it?" he answered, "That's easy! I just say to myself, 'If I was a cow, where would I go?'"

Country schoolboy philosophy that works.

You too have a problem. You've tried every source of help until you are about ready to give up. Advice is cheap, plentiful—and unavailing. Your problem goes too deep for the help of even the most sincere friend. Where can you go?

Applying the schoolboy's simple strategy you can say to yourself, "I am a child of God: a Christian. Where do Christians go for help?" Then go there.

"Where can I go but to the Lord?" asks an old spiritual.

Going to the Lord, telling Him all our problems (as the disciples did when they were troubled) will cause those around us to realize, "She knows where to go."

This is one of the most effective means of witness open to us: knowing where to go in times of stress. While friends and neighbors knock themselves out running from one counseling session to another, we can tell our troubles to the Lord. Observing the peace this brings, others may be led to Him also and may find out "where to go."

HIGH PROTEIN DIET

BIBLE READING: Hebrews 5:12-14

> Let us leave behind the elementary teachings of
> Christ, and advance toward maturity (6:1*a*, Ber-
> keley).

Listen in on the conversation of almost any group of
women and you will probably hear the subject of *diet*. And
"protein" will undoubtedly be part of the vocabulary.

Modern diets—fad and otherwise—have a different goal
than the writer to the Hebrews had in mind. He is making
a bid for *teachers*. (Do we hear a Sunday school super-
intendent sighing, "I know what he is up against.")

Far from finding teacher material, the writer in this
scripture accuses the Christians of childishness and imma-
turity; of being "milk-sucking babies."

"Rather than feed your souls on the meat of the Word
of God that produces mature followers of Christ, you've
been satisfied with infants' food," the writer indicts these
Hebrews.

Grown-up babies! What is sadder than a child who has
never grown, who is stunted either physically or mentally.

Today the Lord would paint for us the picture of a
healthy, well-fed Christian, not only enjoying the blessing
of God, but able to teach others, as against the sorry
spectacle of a "retarded" Christian—voluntarily retarded
due to the choice of diet. Well might we pray:

> Break thou the Bread of Life
> Dear Lord to me.

Then, satisfied, we would offer ourselves as willing teachers,
a joy to our Lord.

WHY ALL THE TROUBLE?

BIBLE READING: Job 5:1-9

Man is born unto trouble, as the sparks fly upward (v. 7).

Since, obviously, a certain measure of trouble comes to each of us, we might think seriously about these words of Socrates (especially if we have ever wished we might trade our troubles):

If all our misfortunes were laid in one common heap whence everyone must take an equal portion, most people would be content to take their own and depart.

God has a purpose in sending trials our way.

"I wish you would pray that I will have more patience," one Christian asks another. "If I do," her friend replied, "I will have to pray you'll have trials, for 'tribulation worketh patience'" (Romans 5:3).

Oliver Wendell Holmes must have understood this truth when he wrote, "If I had a formula for ridding mankind of trouble, I think I would not reveal it, for in doing so, I would do him a dis-service."

That trouble, trials, tribulation, difficulty and sorrow have enriched lives, is amply borne out even in the hymns we so frequently sing. The blind Fanny Crosby, some of whose hymns bless almost every church service we attend; Horatio Spafford, who, after the horror of the devastating Chicago fire, followed by the loss of four daughters in an Atlantic shipwreck, was somehow enabled to write, "It Is Well with My Soul." George Matheson, likewise, threatened by certain blindness and forsaken by a beloved fiancée, gave to us the beautiful, "O Love That Wilt Not Let Me Go."

Although not hymn writers, we can be hymn *singers*, as we recognize God's plan—even when it is spelled t-r-o-u-b-l-e.

WHEN YOU KNOW HIM

BIBLE READING: II Timothy 1:8-12

I know whom I have believed (v. 12).

With some feeling a young woman blurted out, "It's not *what* you know, it's *who* you know that counts!" While we may not know the occasion of her outburst, we have to admit there is truth in what she said, and nowhere is this more true than in the realm of the Spirit.

We can have an acquaintance with some of the world's notable persons; we can claim kinship or friendship with influential people in various areas. Through long hours of study we can know the great men of all time—and still lose out on "who we know."

A young bride remained strangely unimpressed as the names of Plato, Socrates, Aristotle were introduced into the conversation around her table.

"I'm afraid I don't know the philosophies of any of these people," she admitted, then added, "but I know Jesus Christ. I know what He's done for me."

Was she ignorant, this girl who so confidently affirmed, "I know Jesus"? By the world's standards, yes. But so firm was her faith, so secure was she in her knowledge of God, that the guests began to be impressed, not with what she didn't know, but with what she did! One man commented, "I would give my eyeteeth to have one-hundredth of the faith this young woman has."

When you know Him, when you know Him,
You'll love Him just as others do.

And then you'll gladly share your knowledge.

YES—AND NO

BIBLE READING: James 4:1-8

A young mother wrote to a friend, "As well as saying 'yes' graciously, I'm going to have to learn to say 'no' firmly."

Each of us has choices to make in this connection and inevitably some firm "no's" have to be said. Our 1,440 minutes a day can be spent only once. This limitation calls for some "no's" if we would keep from being harried homemakers.

We owe it to our children to learn to say "no"—and mean it.

"Say 'yes,' Mommie," the small charmer pleads. "Please say 'yes.'" But wisdom demands a firm "no."

To the tempter we must say "no" many a time. For this we need more than human resolve and firmness. We need the spiritual stamina that comes only from God as we pray.

The exhortation of today's reading, "Resist the devil," would be tantalizingly impossible without the accompanying "Draw nigh to God and he will draw nigh to you."

In our own strength our "firm no" can be all too easily weakened into a reluctant "yes." We become a prey to Satan's lures.

A popular hymn, "Yield Not to Temptation," holds a clue that helps us to guard against such wiles of the devil:

> Ask the Saviour to help you . . .
> He will carry you through.

He will draw near. Near enough to back up our "no" and make it stick, to back our "yes" until it is accomplished.

DANGER, POISON!

BIBLE READING: II Kings 4:38-41

"Keep out of reach of children," the label on the medicine bottle cautions, and no mother would be indifferent to the warning.

Neither was the Prophet Elisha. He was honestly concerned over the lack of food; anxious that his "theology students" would enjoy a good meal. He didn't dream that the innocent-looking concoction in the big kettle spelled death.

When he learned of the danger he was quick to do something about it.

All around us we see dangerous influences: naked sex on theater marquees, "best sellers" with warped concepts being ladled out by "new theologians." All these spell death.

Oh, it's not the skull-and-crossbones variety of warning. It's a more sophisticated type of poisoning. It is real, nevertheless.

Fortunately for the young men, Elisha knew the antidote and used it in time to save their lives.

We too have at hand the antidote: the pure, unadulterated Word of God in time and in sufficient quantity will save from spiritual death those for whom the Lord holds us responsible.

With all the fine spiritual fare available, we need not fear the world's "poison."

A PERSONAL THING

BIBLE READING: Ezekiel 14:14-20

They shall deliver neither sons nor daughters (v. 16).

We often hear the heartwarming statement, "There's nothing she wouldn't do for her children."

Yet there is one thing no mother, however dedicated and loving, can do for her son or daughter. She can never pass on her own salvation to the members of her family.

Unlike sin, salvation is not hereditary, nor can it be included in a will. While we can pass on to our children almost any possession, each one must reach out and personally appropriate the salvation Christ purchased with His blood on the cross.

God plucks from the pages of history the names of three outstanding Bible personalities, citing them as examples. Surely the message is clear. If these—mighty in faith and obedience—can by no means include their families in their own salvation experience, how can we hope to do so? (Have you noted the *repetition* of the warning?)

How vital it is then that we seek by every means at our disposal to lead our children to Christ, to make certain they are not depending on anyone's faith but their own!

Opportunities to do this come sometimes in unique ways. A little fellow who was a keen fisherman heard a pastor read the scripture, "Where their worm dieth not" (Mark 9:44). He pricked up his ears. He was interested in worms. Listening, he determined he was not going to the hell the pastor was describing, not if he could do anything about it! And that night, as he asked questions, his mother pointed him to the Saviour who came to save him from such a fate. Now salvation is a personal thing to him.

117

THE ONLY ONE

BIBLE READING: Luke 9:49-56

A pastor, greeting a visitor at his church, heard this story: "Pastor, I came here for one reason. Last Sunday I listened to your service on the radio and heard you farewell your daughter. I said to myself, 'I've met a lot of ministers who have sent other people's sons and daughters to the mission field, but I want to meet this man whose own girl has gone.' Am I right that she is your only daughter?"

There is something warm, human, to which we all can relate in Luke's account of Jairus' only daughter and the widow of Nain's only son (Luke 7:12). Notice the paramount interest the Lord Jesus showed in their dire circumstances.

We are reminded too of Abraham's only son (Genesis 22:2). How great the loss when the only child is taken. How blessed beyond words must it have been to have that son, that daughter, restored—alive! (A pastor, searching the New Testament for a message for a funeral, found that Jesus had broken up every funeral He ever attended!) The compassionate Christ brought life out of death.

Is it not all the more significant then, that we read:

> He that spared not his own Son, but delivered him up for us all (Romans 8:32a).

Can we contemplate upon this without immediately thinking of John 3:16:

> For God so loved the world that he gave his only begotten Son.

And can our response be other than "Thank You, Lord"?

SOME THINGS DON'T CHANGE

BIBLE READING: I John 1:1

That which was from the beginning (v. 1).

Former Prime Minister of Britain, Harold Macmillan, speaking of the new nations emerging in Africa, coined the phrase, "winds of change."

We homemakers are well aware of constant change: newspapers, radio and television, salesmen calling at our door, supermarket shelves, these all scream "change." We would be blind and insensitive, though, if we did not recognize these "winds of change" in many other areas of our lives.

Even so, some things do not change. Sin, for example. Sin is "from the beginning." An astute Christian once remarked, "Sin does not die of old age." True. Neither does it change basically. The boasted "New Morality" is the age-old *im*morality—with a new name. God's standard has not changed.

An encouraging trend is that opportunities for witness have changed, for the better. The space age lends itself to a questing spirit: "Where is heaven?" is being asked as astronauts probe outer space. And over a cup of coffee, we can take the opportunity to give specific directions on how to reach heaven: the same, changeless "I am the way" (John 14:6).

To the questioning soul who has known the way but has somehow wandered into sin, the way back is the changeless:

If we confess our sins, he is faithful and just to forgive us our sins (I John 1:9).

The Christian in need of the assurance of Christ's presence need only whisper,

O Thou, who changest not, abide with me.

YOU'RE NOT LISTENING

BIBLE READING: Exodus 3:4-9

I have . . . heard their cry (v. 7).

"Mother! You're not listening," five-year-old Tim complains.

"I'm busy, son," his mother answers.

"God's busy—and *He* listens," retorted Tim.

His mother "got the message." It started her thinking. Is my little boy right? Do I really not listen? The conviction made a new person out of her. Instead of the almost incessant chatterer she was, she became a deliberate listener. After a while she agreed heartily with Ernest Hemingway in his statement: "I like to listen. I have learned a great deal from listening carefully. Most people never listen."

Listening—not continually talking—to God became a fixed habit. Her list of "give me's" grew shorter. Reverent quiet before God produced a calm spirit within her.

The "payoff" came the day her Tim admitted, with an adoring smile: "Mommy, it's nice telling you things. You listen to me."

If "silence is golden," then listening must be some form of refined gold that beautifies the "wearer." It brings rewards other than those mentioned by Hemingway.

It may be that you feel inadequate to serve God as a Sunday school teacher, speaker at women's meetings, president of the women's group, or such forms of service. Do you realize you can be a listener and serve Him well?

A noted Christian psychologist has said, "No one will ever get well until he can talk out his troubles." They need a listener. Are you available? Or "too busy"?

FOR THE TEEN-AGER'S MOM

BIBLE READING: Romans 5:1-8

The love of God is shed abroad in our hearts (v. 5).

Whatever our personal reaction to the word "teen-ager," the army of 13-to-19-year-olds is a powerful force in our generation. They are the victims of pressures we never knew. New fears confront them. New challenges face them.

If we would sincerely desire to have a healthy, mutually worthwhile relationship with teens these few proven tips might be worth our pondering:

DO be sympathetic, DON'T be cynical.

DO show concern, DON'T be condemning.

DO pray, DON'T pry.

Simple? Yes, but amazingly effective when practiced consistently.

A Christian mother who took these "do's and don'ts" to heart was agreeably surprised one day when a neighbor admitted: "I watch you and your girls together. How I wish Cindy and I got along even half as well. You seem to do and say just the right thing."

"I try," the girls' mother replied, "but I just know that if I didn't take time to pray for my girls—and myself— every day, I'd be a dismal failure. I ask God to make me an understanding mother."

Realizing how much Christ has done for us, we will want to let His love shine out in our lives—out to the teen-agers.

THE GOLDEN RULE FOR IN-LAWS

BIBLE READING: Ruth 2:19-23

She . . . dwelt with her mother in law (v. 23*b*).

Introducing a visitor, a minister said, "I'd like you to meet my brother-in-law, and my brother-in-grace." Then he added, "The latter takes care of the former."

In-laws! The time-honored butt of jokes: the prime examples of human incompatibility.

"Your house all shined up and the baking done?" a neighbor inquired when she heard of the imminent arrival of the mother-in-law next door.

"Yes, *that's* done. Now I'm getting all prayed up," admitted the young "in-law." "Phil's mother gets me so irked, no matter how hard I try to get along with her, that I just thought I'd better pray a lot before she gets here."

No "Ruth-and-Naomi" relationship here, obviously. No "whither thou goest, I will go; and where thou lodgest I will lodge" (Ruth 1:16).

But the young wife had learned a secret: a "Golden Rule" for getting along with in-laws. Praying—especially if we pray for ourselves as in-laws with whom the other person has to cope—cannot but result in smoother, happier relationships.

Do we perhaps tend to think of the Ruth and Naomi situation as idealistic and forget that the sound basis was spiritual? These two women worshiped a common God in a day when idol worship was at its height. It was Ruth's putting her trust "under the wings" of the Lord (2:12) that created the bond.

It may be that we too can profitably examine and improve our spiritual relationship with our in-laws.

IS YOUR MOTIVE SHOWING?

BIBLE READING: Esther 8:1-6

How can I endure to see . . . the destruction of my
kindred? (v. 6).

Have you listened to prayer requests that sound something like this: "Please pray for my husband. It would be
so nice; so much more pleasant at home if only he were a
believer"? (Perhaps the ashtrays or drinking glasses are a
source of embarrassment when company comes.)

Others pray with the utmost sincerity of motive, their
sole concern that the loved one be saved for his own sake:
to enjoy the peace of God here, and all eternity in the presence of the Saviour. Such people just can't bear to think of
a loved one being lost.

There is no questioning Queen Esther's motive. This
presumptuous, fervent plea is ample evidence, in a culture
where even a queen dare not approach uninvited into the
king's presence.

"I can't endure to see the evil that will come to my people." There is a desperate pathos in her words; fitting ac-
companiment for her determination, "If I perish, I perish"
(4:16).

Elevation to the throne had not made her one bit less
conscious of her own people's plight. She could have no
peace or happiness, safe in the palace, while their lives were
in jeopardy. Her very desperation lent ardor to her plea.
It reminds us of the hymn "I Am Praying for You":

And now He is watching in tenderness o'er me,
But oh, that my Savior were *your Savior, too*.

There's no mistaking the motive here.

FOR THE PASTOR'S WIFE

BIBLE READING: Matthew 25:34-40

I was a stranger and you entertained Me (v. 35*b*, Berkeley).

Meet Peggy, the pastor's wife. One day she awakened with the pleasant thought, "I have this whole day to myself," and in her mind she planned all the things she had long wanted to do when she had a free day.

That was before the doorbell rang. The next hour she spent listening to a woman's problems. (Just as if I were "Dear Abby," she said to herself.) But her face glowed with interest and, before the woman left, the pastor's wife was genuinely sympathetic and anxious to help.

No sooner had the caller gone than the telephone interrupted the planned schedule. "Can I ask you to pray with me about ......?" And the prayer request was explained in detail.

Eating her lunch, Peggy was again disturbed, this time by her husband calling from the church where a conference was in progress for the local pastors.

"Honey," he began, "do you think you can put four extra plates on for supper? I just heard of a family whose home was burned." Listening, Peggy was mentally surveying the refrigerator and planning what items she could easily give to the distressed family.

"My free day," she thought with a wry smile.

Late in the afternoon an excited voice on the phone brought unexpected reward: "Remember that time I called and asked you to pray about a bad situation in our family? Well, I just want you to know that everything's all right. I just had to call and tell you."

"Thank You, Lord," prayed the pastor's wife, "for planning this 'free day' for me, Your way."

TO GOD FOR CHRISTMAS

BIBLE READING: Isaiah 12:1-6

Sing unto the LORD; for he hath done excellent things (v. 5).

It was Christmas Eve. The church was crowded. Suddenly the young soloist felt her knees begin to shake. Her number was next on the program.

"I can't—I'll never make it, I'm *so* nervous," she wailed inwardly. But moments later her rich contralto voice rang out to thrill the audience as she sang, "He Shall Feed His Flock Like a Shepherd."

In the New Year's Eve testimony service she confessed, "I panicked when I realized it was time for my solo. I don't know why. I just felt I couldn't go through with it. Then I began to think about what Christmas really is: that it's Jesus' birthday. So I prayed silently: 'Lord Jesus, I'm scared. You know I am, but I would like to sing this to You—for a birthday present.' Then I wasn't scared anymore."

A song of praise for a Christmas gift to God: a birthday present to Jesus our Saviour.

We too can put the Lord Jesus on our Christmas list. Perhaps we can't all be soloists, but we can sing a hymn of praise—or let our lives be the hymn.

"God *is* my salvation," verse 2 clearly states. What better time than Christmas to say "Thank you" to God in some way.

Aren't you glad that your "song unto the Lord" sounds musical to Him, though you may feel you "can't carry a tune in a bucket." So—let's remember that birthday present!

TIRED, TIRED, TIRED

BIBLE READING: Isaiah 40:28-31

He imparts vigor to the fainting (v. 29a, Berkeley).

"But I'm so tired all the time!" Increasingly we hear not only older, but young women—and some of them Christians —bemoan, "I haven't any pep. I'm tired all the time." This in spite of all the vim, vigor and vitality pills!

Wouldn't it be a good time to heed Isaiah's advice and "Wait on the Lord"?

Just how does one "wait on the Lord"? We all know about waiting for a kettle to boil or a husband to come home for dinner. (We do this with foot-tapping impatience.)

"Waiting on the Lord" means spending time in His presence: in His Word. No reading the verse for the day from the calendar then dropping on one knee with a I - hope - You're - ready - to - listen - Lord - for - I - have - a - hundred - things - to - do - today attitude of heart.

But think of the returns we get for the time spent with God.

We "mount up with the wings as eagles": go with flying colors through some difficult experience that calls for all we have. We become a testimony to all who see us. And we don't use up all our strength in doing it.

"Run and not be weary": we have a sufficient reserve to run around and accomplish the many duties that call us— and still not be "played out."

"Walk and not faint": oh, there's where we so often fail. We manage to rise to the big occasion. It's the "walking," the daily grind, the wearing routine that gets us down. Then isn't it worth waiting for strength for flying, running, walking. And never getting tired?

THERE IS NO SUBSTITUTE

BIBLE READING: Exodus 12:1-13

The blood was the sign, Lord,
That marked them for Thine, Lord.

Napoleon Bonaparte stood one day in his map room in the city of Fontainebleau, and, indicating a dot on the map, he stormed, "We could conquer all of Europe but for that red spot." The "red spot" was England.

The Death Angel could touch every home in Egypt except for the "red spots."

Joshua's conquering army, with the help of the Lord, could touch every home in Jericho—except the one with the scarlet line: the "red spot" (Joshua 2:21).

No substitute would have been effective. The scarlet line was the sign agreed upon. No substitute—not a living lamb (or a blood donation for a worthy cause) would have sufficed.

We've been thinking about salt, in this little book. Again we can draw an analogy. The ambulance roars up to the door marked "EMERGENCY," and an ever-alert team goes into action. Invariably included as a part of the stock emergency preparation is a supply of saline solution to correct the salt imbalance that could endanger a life.

No substitute is used.

In these days when "new theology," "man's progress toward God" and kindred humanistic substitutes are offered to the unwary, the eternal truth rings out: "When I see the blood"—not the blood of "a lamb on Jewish altars slain"—but the blood of the "Lamb of God, which taketh away the sin of the world" (John 1:29).

There is no substitute.

SPRINKLE AS NEEDED

BIBLE READING: II Kings 2:19-22

Cast the salt in (v. 21, Berkeley).

We hear much these days about water pollution. Elisha, in the city of Jericho, was faced with the same situation: a "pleasant city," but unfit water. What did he do? He threw in some salt.

It's important that salt be used just where and how it is needed. For example, while some areas of the world (California, for instance) are using complex machinery to desalt the water and provide a fresh supply, other countries (Pakistan) are diligently building vats to hold salt water. As the sun pours down on it, the water is evaporated and the salt then shipped to needy places.

So we, "the salt of the earth," must ever ask God to show us where He would have us to be and what He would have us to do, if we would be effective for Him.

Job asked the practical question, "Can that which is unsavoury be eaten without salt?" (6:6).

We would not willfully withhold the salt, the seasoning that would make our witness palatable. Neither should we use up our supply where it is already plentiful. To quote a missionary statesman of our own day, Dr. Oswald J. Smith, "Why should anyone hear the gospel *twice* before everyone has heard it once?"

As we earnestly pray, the Lord will direct us to where He knows "salt" is needed. Living close to Him, our "saltshaker" will be kept well filled.

Happy, profitable salt sprinkling!